CONTENTS AT A GLANCE

TABLE OF CONTENTS

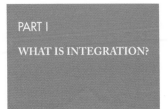

PART I

WHAT IS INTEGRATION?

PART II

INTEGRATION
PRIMER FOR THE
PROGRAMMATICALLY
INCLINED

PART III

INTEGRATION
PRIMER FOR THE
ARTISTICALLY INCLINED

Dedication

For Michael, the most creative spirit I know.

About the Author

 A writer, instructor, and designer, **Molly E. Holzschlag** brings attitude and enthusiasm to books, magazines, classrooms, and web sites. Honored by Webgrrls as one of the Top 25 Most Influential Women on the web, Molly has spent more than a decade working in the online world. She has written 20 books on HTML and web design and development topics, including the best-selling *Special Edition Using HTML 4.0* and the internationally acclaimed *Web by Design*.

Her popular column of two and a half years, "Integrated Design," appeared monthly in the internationally popular *WebTechniques Magazine* until the magazine's closing in early 2002. Molly served for a year as the executive editor of *Web Review*, and she has contributed features and columns to Adobe Studios, Adobe.com, Builder.com, Digital Chicago, Digital New York, IBM developerWorks, *MacWorld*, *MSDN*, *PC Magazine*, and other developer publications.

When offline, Molly plays guitar and sings in the original acoustic duo Courage Sisters. For books, giveaways, training, speaking events, and other items of fun and interest, drop by her web site: **www.molly.com**.

About the Technical Editors

Steven Champeon is the CTO of hesketh.com, a web-services firm in Raleigh, NC that specializes in distinctive B2B and corporate sites, vibrant online communities, and high-impact applications. He has provided technical editing on the topics of XML, XHTML, and other web-related topics, and he was the development editor for Jeffrey Veen's best-seller, *The Art and Science of Web Design*, published by New Riders. In addition to his work as an editor, Champeon is a frequent contributor to online and print magazines for web professionals, and he is the author of *Building Dynamic HTML GUIs*.

A highly sought-after speaker at trade conferences, Champeon regularly participates in CMP's web conference circuit and Cool Site in a Day competition, Thunder Lizard, South by Southwest, and others, often speaking on DHTML and how to grow successful online communities.

Steve Romaniello is an artist, writer, and educator who has been involved in digital graphics for more than a decade. A professor at Pima Community College in Tucson, Arizona, Steve conducts seminars in digital and web graphics, both nationally and internationally. He is CEO of GlobalEye Systems, a software training and consulting provider. Steve is also the author of *Mastering Photoshop 6* and the instructor in Sybex's interactive *Photoshop 6 Learning Studio*.

Acknowledgments

This book has been in the works for more than two years. It began as a conversation in San Francisco with New Riders Executive Editor Steve Weiss. The conversation carried across time and location; follow-up discussions occurred in Indiana, California, and, of course, online.

So, the first acknowledgment in this book must be for Steve, who believed in me—and my ideas—enough to give me the opportunity to write in a more rarified air than usual. For this opportunity I am eternally grateful.

From New Riders, I would like to thank Development Editor Barb Terry, Designer Wil Cruz, and the production and copy editors who helped see the book through to fruition.

My literary agent, David Fugate of Waterside Productions, is a great friend indeed. Maureen Maloney keeps my authoring logistics in order, and for her attentiveness and expedience I am very thankful.

Content-wise, Julie Sullivan organized the research efforts that went into this book. From a developmental and technical perspective, Steve Champeon provided intelligent, thoughtful support, and I'm grateful for his ongoing influence in my work. Designer Amy Burnham worked with me to create a general look and feel for the book that was fresh and unique, and that could be easily modified and enhanced by Wil's own vision.

To my family, friends, and especially my readers, I simply want to say thank you for your blessings of love and kindness.

A Message from New Riders

As the reader of this book, you are our most important critic and commentator. We value your opinion and want to know what we're doing right, what we could do better, in what areas you'd like to see us publish, and any other words of wisdom you're willing to pass our way.

As Executive Editor at New Riders, I welcome your comments. You can fax, email, or write me directly to let me know what you did or didn't like about this book—as well as what we can do to make our books better. When you write, please be sure to include this book's title, ISBN, and author, as well as your name and phone or fax number. I will carefully review your comments and share them with the authors and editors who worked on the book.

Please note that I cannot help you with technical problems related to the topic of this book, and that due to the high volume of email I receive, I might not be able to reply to every message. Thanks.

Fax   317-581-4663

Email: **steve.weiss@newriders.com**

Mail: Steve Weiss
          Executive Editor
          New Riders Publishing
          201 West 103rd Street
          Indianapolis, IN 46290 USA

Visit Our Web Site: www.newriders.com

On our web site, you'll find information about our other books, the authors we partner with, book updates and file downloads, promotions, discussion boards for online interaction with other users and with technology experts, and a calendar of trade shows and other professional events with which we'll be involved. We hope to see you around.

Email Us from Our Web Site

Go to **www.newriders.com** and click on the Contact Us link if you…

- Have comments or questions about this book.

- Want to report errors that you have found in this book.

- Have a book proposal or are interested in writing for New Riders.

- Would like us to send you one of our author kits.

- Are an expert in a computer topic or technology and are interested in being a reviewer or technical editor.

- Want to find a distributor for our titles in your area.

- Are an educator/instructor who wants to preview New Riders books for classroom use. In the body/comments area, include your name, school, department, address, phone number, office days/hours, text currently in use, and enrollment in your department, along with your request for either desk/ examination copies or additional information.

Introduction

The shelves are crowded with books on the technology and art of creating web sites. These books tend to highlight a given technology or approach, but very few provide solutions that encourage balancing technical skill with aesthetic instinct. Yet without this balance, web builders working on the client side are severely limited in their abilities to improve their sites. Visually skilled designers may be expected to make heavy markup changes; technically skilled designers may be forced to attempt various designs to attract clients. Because of this need for integrated skills in their jobs, web builders must quickly acquire abilities and learn concepts for which they may have little training or inclination.

For three years I wrote a popular column for *Web Techniques Magazine* called "Integrated Design." In this column, I focused on client-side integration of markup languages and visual design concerns. The goal was to encourage technically savvy web builders, who tend to be more "left-brained," to think aesthetically and to get more visual web builders, the "right-brainers," to think technically. This creates the potential for you to integrate your knowledge effectively so as to create great web sites and also gain a more profound perspective about how the web works. The result of this holistic thinking in turn allows for innovation. Once you gain this perspective, you will be empowered to work not only as a technician or designer, but also as a strategist at the highest level. You will understand the precise—and the global.

How This Book Is Structured

Integrated Design is divided into three sections. Part I sets the stage for integrated learning by examining educational challenges, learning theory, and case studies that demonstrate the power of an integrated approach. Then, the book goes right to the heart of integration: Using the language that is most familiar to each, the chapters teach designers and client-side programmers the tools of the trade in clear form. For programmers, Part II lays out the fundamentals of visual design in the context of technology. You will examine the *technology* of color, shape, space, and typography. Theory is combined with hands-on exercises. In Part III, more visual learners are taught markup, style, and scripting technologies, coming at the challenge from the perspective of what you know best—design. Hands-on examples of how to effectively employ technology or design methods to achieve a specific goal help to integrate the learning.

Along the way, compelling "Integrated Exercises" will strengthen your logical and creative thinking. Drawn from psychological, sociological, scientific, and creative process resources, these activities encourage you to get away from the computer and participate in the natural, organic world—where, of course, the fundamentals of technology and design are born. You will also find helpful Notes, Tips, and Cautions sprinkled throughout the book, as well as interesting quotes from people inside and outside the web industry.

The main idea of this book is to inspire new ways of thinking *about* what we do as web designers and developers, rather than the actual things we do. *Integrated Design* is ultimately a process, the end result being a deeper understanding not just of the *how* of technology and design, but most especially, the *why*.

Who Should Read This Book

Integrated Design is geared for professional web builders looking to broaden their perspectives about the web and the work it entails. The book assumes a basic knowledge of HTML or XHTML web markup and basic graphic production skills with such imaging software as Adobe Photoshop.

Typical readers for this book will have at least a year of experience building web sites using markup and graphics, but perhaps aren't aware of recommended practices. Or, they are challenged by the limitations of prior education and focus on specialization versus integration. Other readers interested in this book will be server-side programmers, security specialists, print designers, and others attempting to improve client-side development skills or transition completely into web design as a primary activity.

PART I

What Is Integration?

CHAPTER 1

Challenges to Web Builders

The cool factor is dead. Certain dreams are buried in ash. The web is more than 10 years old, but despite the difficulties of these contemporary times, it is still thriving. The web remains vibrant.

As framers of the web, we must ask, "Where have we been?" Of course, the more obvious concern is where the future will take us, but that discussion will ensue as this book progresses. We now have enough information to begin viewing what we did in the context of the past so that we can make the best use of our lessons learned.

I recently looked back at some of my old writings and found that, in a book that I wrote in 1995, I proposed that web design would soon shift from a one-man-band scenario to an orchestral model. It is hard to imagine that the one-man-band web designer model was not only possible but actually prevalent back then. Even that early on, it was becoming clear that the web would demand an awful lot of us, asking us to learn new technologies as well as new ways of thinking and working. Balancing a range of skills became increasingly important to our success.

It was evident that skill integration would become crucial as early as 1993, when the Mosaic browser provided a visual glimpse at the web's wiry undergrowth (see Figure 1.1). But even then, it took a few years for web development to take a more structured professional shape. Mostly, we were experimenting—attempting to combine HTML, graphics, and eventually scripts to make sites do cool things. By 1995, the need for a professional approach to creating web sites became clear.

In 1995, web professionals came from a wide range of backgrounds: They were programmers; systems administrators; SGML document conversion operators; artists; media specialists in TV, radio, and advertising; businesspeople; writers; and general enthusiasts. We all came to the field with a lot of energy, and we brought experience from these other realms. Web design excited us because it was a new frontier that was challenging to different parts of our personalities and skills, was full of attitude, and was exciting because it was—and still remains—completely new and ever changing.

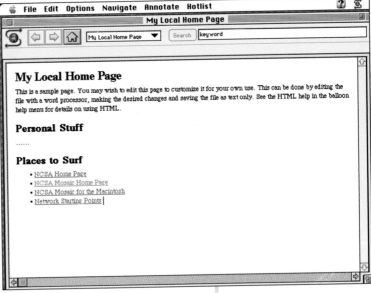

Figure 1.1   The Mosaic browser: a very simple, early design.

Those of us who were captivated by the web early on worked hard to learn what we could. The simplistic nature of web technologies at that time pushed certain people to create really innovative designs that relied on simplicity (see Figure 1.2). Limitations often spur innovation, and the early days of the web proved it (see Figure 1.3).

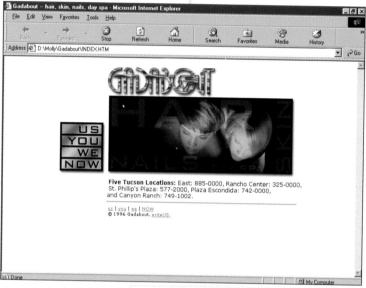

Figure 1.2   Simplicity spurs innovation. Compare the simple look in Figure 1.1
to this still simple but much more visual approach, circa 1996,
and compare that with today's very different approach, found in
Figure 1.3.

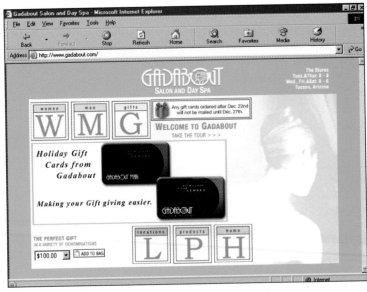

Figure 1.3 *In many ways, visual design on the web has become more complex.*

Soon thereafter, scripting and style came onto the client-side scene. Designers suddenly were writing scripts, and programmers started thinking about presentation or began examining motion graphics for the web. This integration was a difficult process, and for many good reasons. As adult learners, we have largely been inhibited, not empowered, by the way we are taught. This appears to cross cultural boundaries, too, although the reasons sometimes are cultural and sometimes are made problematic by a lack of access to advanced education and resources.

These inhibitions are often powerfully imprinted upon us. I have an anecdote from my childhood that illustrates this point. When I was a young girl learning multiplication tables, I hit a brick wall computing anything higher than multiples of 5. I innocently asked my teacher (I went to parochial school) for help and was told in dulcet tones not to worry because I'd "have no need for that" when I grew up.

Despite my growing independent spirit, I was raised to respect authority, and at that young age, I did. I knew that something was wrong with the scenario—I just didn't know what. I went back to my desk and hid my tears as I made an honest struggle to learn the information, but I still found myself failing.

Later I learned in no uncertain terms that the inhibition born of that experience would cripple me for a time in very painful ways. I had to relearn math as an adult and also make hard choices about my career interests based on an honest evaluation of whether I'd ever gain the math skills I needed. At one time I was interested in pursuing a career in genetics and virology. I made it through the first few years of a premed program before I realized that it was just too great of a struggle.

By nature, I'm a verbal person. Every academic and personality test I've ever taken has shown this to be true. But I am not lacking in logic, and I am certainly not lacking in analytical skills. I suspect that many of us are the same: Although we display our strengths and weaknesses differently, we have to work that much harder to achieve understanding in those realms if our weaknesses are not strengthened.

I suspect that most education rewards our performance but passes off or negates our efforts in areas in which we do not excel. This practice is pedagogically wrong. In simple terms, to teach children to embrace only their strengths and to ignore or even feel shame about their weaknesses is absurd. I prefer this approach: Give children ample opportunity to learn everything. Where they appear weaker, spend extra time nurturing them. I am absolutely certain that most basically intelligent youngsters will break through barriers much more effectively early on. Ideally, we should be looking at our education systems and demanding reform.

But here we are: We're adults, and we are being asked by the web environment to use our skills and our minds in ways or to extremes that we've never been asked to use or challenge them. So how do we proceed? What do we do? It's not as if we have so much time in our busy lives to learn not only the technology *du jour,* but also fill in all the components that we're missing—for me it's programming, and for others it's visual aesthetics.

Fragmentation

Part of the web builder's problem now is trying to work out these difficulties. A range of things have occurred to do that, including using project managers and combining the skills of a graphic designer with a programmer. And some very good emerging techniques and methods can help this process.

However, I think that, out of fear and necessity, the industry has changed—and it has changed us. Skill integration worked well until the skills necessary to build a professional web page multiplied beyond the juggling point. Over the past few years, many maturing web developers have set aside integrated techniques and looked more closely at various specialties. This could involve focusing on the client side, becoming a great HTML author, a content specialist, a JavaScript and DHTML guru, or an innovative designer. On the server side, countless languages and development opportunities are arising. This could mean focusing on application languages such as Java, database technologies for the web, or a range of other applications. Some of us moved away from the skill integration that had defined our working identities to that point, and we sought new careers by defaulting to specialization.

Many of us are still struggling with this process. It's especially hard for those of us who successfully integrated our skills in the early days to pinpoint what we now want to specialize in. Just because you like visual design doesn't mean that programming isn't a passion, too. As a result, circumstances often push us toward the specialty that best satisfies a dictated need. Of course, others' needs don't necessarily reflect our own passions. On a personal level, many designers feel that specialization has dimmed some of the joy and sense of accomplishment that they once felt.

http://size-isnt-everything.co.uk

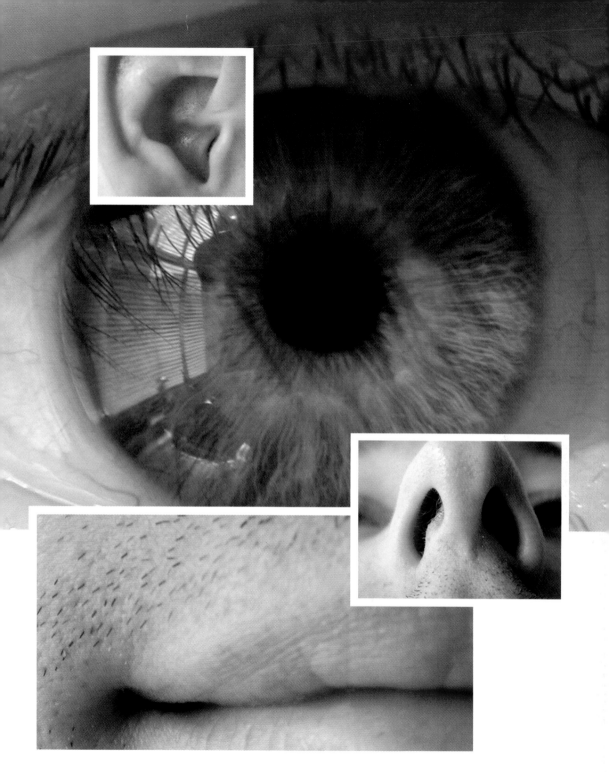

http://size-isnt-everything.co.uk

Specialization

On a larger scale, has fragmentation assisted or encumbered us? Is such deep specialization good for the industry and the people who propel the web? I argue that it's not. Let's use the medical field as an example: If you're going for medical care, at least in the United States, you're likely to first consult a primary care physician. After that, you're shuttled off to the specialist, who then hones in on the specific problem.

The fatal flaw with this method is that the specialist doesn't know you, or doesn't have the full experience of your strengths and weaknesses. In effect, the specialist can provide a solution to a particular problem, but that solution might not be a perfect fit for your overall situation. In medicine, a lot of unfortunate mistakes occur precisely because a specialist is looking at the problem, not the person.

Web design and development face the same risks. It has become increasingly clear that no one person can do all of this stuff. However, if we forget to look at the project as a whole—if we fail to work to integrate our own skills, no matter what our official "position" in the field is—the health of web design and development will suffer.

Integration: Part Two

Here enters the project manager, who oversees specialty integration. Although I'm seeing more literature about web project management, the field is still emerging. A project manager needs considerable breadth of industry knowledge, some depth of knowledge, and most certainly communication skills that will link the now fragmented web development departments.

To put it simply, we still need integration. But now, instead of integrating our own skills, we're integrating those of a combined team. Web design and development specialists flounder without someone to successfully orchestrate a given project.

Unfortunately, integration is becoming harder, primarily because of the explosive interest in wireless and alternative device design. These devices add an entirely new layer of rich but complex technology, and their design needs are often distinctly different than what we've learned to address for the web. Consider that a technical specifications listing for a web designer or developer might include such things as knowing HTML, Perl/CGI, Java, Photoshop, Illustrator, and .NET, as well as being an expert database developer. In recent years, new specialties have been added: usability, information architecture specialists, accessibility specialists, legal specialists, and of course, web marketing.

Sobering, isn't it? Only a few years after specialization took over, we seem to be at another crossroads. In the aftershocks of our industry shakeup, how will the demands of integration and specialization influence our projects and the way we work over time?

In my mind, it really boils down to three choices:

- We can work on a self-selected series of technologies and integrate them into our skill sets.

- We can decide to specialize in one specific topic.

- We can let our employers' needs guide us.

I think that the complexity of the demands on all of us clearly demonstrates the quandary we're in. Although we've come a long way, it's most definitely time to take a careful look at what we're doing with our careers. Okay, so you don't have to wax as philosophical as I do. Still, you can decide exactly what kind of developer or designer you want to be.

The Past as Context

Looking at our past sheds some light not only on how we can work more effectively today, but also on how we might prepare for tomorrow's unknowns. We're at a defining moment in our industry, one that has been ushered in with some unfortunate doom and gloom. In recent times, many of us (or our colleagues) have lost or changed jobs, and the entire industry has been experiencing a profound shift.

Although this shift is unpleasant, it is also necessary. Look at it as a correction, if you will, similar to what the stock market does every so often. And although countless people have lost jobs, there's little doubt in my mind that those people who are serious about long-term careers with web and related technologies will land on their feet.

Despite the fragmentation of our industry, the web designers and developers who will be most empowered, most able to find good jobs and contracts, and most able to adapt to our industry's rapid change are the ones with integrated, diverse skills. Even if you're specializing, I am convinced that you will still need integration.

Teams and Individuals

Work teams historically have functioned by distinguishing roles. Designers are responsible for graphics, while programmers and developers produce code and functionality. This separation appeals to managers for numerous reasons: personality difficulties, rapid application development belief systems, and the need to delegate tasks efficiently. This model works, but integrating the components at the end of the process can be time-consuming and unwieldy.

While many web development companies are working to gain better integration, in many cases there's little or no real communication between team members who work by strict task guidelines. Separation inhibits our individual and contributory strengths. How can I, as a designer or programmer, ever be given an opportunity to link programming concepts and design concepts effectively if I'm segregated from my team members? As a result of this separation, we lose potential innovation.

Our education often teaches us that we are either creative or scientific, and never the twain shall meet. Employers extend that model, separating artistic duties from technical tasks. But how employees identify themselves significantly impacts the production process. Pigeonholing them isn't an effective way to produce quality work.

Steven Champeon, respected speaker, writer, and CTO of hesketh.com/inc. (see Figure 1.4), points out that there's as much creativity in programming and technology as in visual design:

> *Programmers aren't creative? Designers aren't serious? Please. Programming is as artistic an activity as playing with colors and shapes. Just because programming isn't primarily visual doesn't mean it's not creative or artistic. Sure, you do have to be conscious of the rules of syntax, but any halfway decent designer who doesn't take the constraints of his or her medium into account isn't doing design—they're just playing with colors and shapes.*

Champeon favors a broader perspective: "Please don't perpetuate the silly split between visuals and hard-core techies any more than is necessary."

He has a point, and it's an enlightened one. It's rare to hear that design and programming are similar activities. After all, as I've mentioned, western education divides people into one of two camps: liberal arts or science and technology. From the earliest points in our education, we are encouraged to follow our strengths rather than challenge our weaknesses. By the time we start working, we've been successfully pigeonholed as a "creative type" or a "techie."

If we actually look at what design and programming require, there's a lot of overlap. Both are acts of creativity and precision if you're doing them well. Both require a range of skills. Whether you're designing or writing a program, a group of peers oversees your production process.

Pulling colorful order from design chaos is no different than making logical, bug-free programs from the same chaos. Designers must not only understand color, shape, space, and typography, but also how to use complex tools to achieve results. Similarly, programmers must understand the component parts of programming as well as a range of tools. A well-written program is as elegant as a well-designed visual composition. In essence, designers and programmers do the same things in context, but it is the content that is the major difference.

>>HIRE US
>>WORK HERE
>>LOGIN

ABOUT   NEWS

Steven Champeon

Chief Technology Officer

Steven's status as a recognized subject matter expert in a number of technical disciplines speaks to the experience and know-how he brings to his role as CTO. A well-written and well-connected member of the diverse community that "weaves the Web," Steven is frequently invited to speak at industry conferences and other national events. In keeping his finger on the pulse of the Web industry, Steven is able to ensure that hesketh.com stays on the cutting edge of emerging technology and trends. Just as important, though, is his foundation in the enduring principles of good coding, design, and information architecture.

Speaking schedule

Most Recently at South by SouthWest, Austin TX. March, 2002
Topics: Non-traditional web design, community, dHTML.

hesketh.com

Expertise   Process   Proof

Vision

To craft, deliver, support, and inspire flexible, elegant web solutions emphasizing vision and creativity and fostering positive relationships.

The client is the cornerstone of our business. Our clients are involved in the process of development, and we create lasting relationships.

Values
commitment, persistence, honesty and integrity, fun, passion, service, harmony and balance, intelligence, and craftsmanship

Related items
Vision
Team
Culture
Community
Profile
History
Careers
Contact

We seek appropriate uses of technology for each client rather than choosing a solution based solely on what's new, hot, or exciting.

We demonstrate excellence — professionally, personally, and through the sites we build.

hesketh.com is a lifestyle company. We provide continuity and a lasting and satisfying work environment. We are a partner our clients can rely on year after year.

hesketh.com has a highly collaborative team atmosphere. Teams find the work interesting; so much so that it's a joy to do. And the company is a place where individuals working in teams can fully get into their zone, reveling in the flow of the work.

hesketh.com is involved in local, professional, and online communities.

hesketh.com

Expertise   Process   Proof

Culture

Integrated Space — creative, open, and designed for intelligent interaction

The hesketh.com corporate culture inspires creativity and a bold use of technology. Team collaborations accomplish sophisticated results. Individual talents add flare to each design.

Related items
Vision
Team
Culture
Community
Profile
History
Careers
Contact

Our integrated workspace advances the concepts of collaborative exchange while encouraging personal reflection. Private offices ring a large work area, which may be customized several times a day depending on the needs of individual projects.

hesketh.com

Expertise   Process   Proof

ARE YOU READY?
ARE YOU SURE?

$20 billion a year is left on the table due to poor usability

35% of users leave frustrating sites for competitors' sites

"Thank you! We knew it could be done--we just didn't know where to begin to automate it."
Joanna Wolfe, Webmaster, OUP

CTO Steve Champeon's next book has been released, Cascading Style Sheets: Separating Content from Presentation, Published by glasshaus, Ltd.

Our latest project races to life in the fast paced world of Formula car racing. Buckle up. Read the press release. See the site. Hold on to your hat.

Read CTO Steve Champeon's latest article, Why DHTML Will Win, now online in this month's New Architect.

Figure 1.4 **www.hesketh.com** *works to choose integrated teams who communicate across boundaries.*

The Need for Hybrid Personalities

Not only is stereotyping employees a detriment to the work that they, as individuals, output or feel passion for, but it also undermines the needs and goals of team members. Many people working on web teams already are finding that they like sampling different tasks from both the programming and the design sides. Alan Richmond, creator of the *Web Developer's Virtual Library* (now with encyclozine), has this to say:

> *A good site isn't built only by brilliant programmers, or by talented graphic artists, or by lucid content authors, or by insightful managers. It will be built by their synergy, each one respecting the contributions of the others, and feeding off them for the inspiration for their own creativity. Building the web is a collaboration at all levels.*

These individuals have been referred to as "hybrids." To my way of thinking, they are *integrationists*, people who have succeeded to some degree in integrating a range of skills that might not overtly appear complimentary but that ultimately are. Integrationists are often at the forefront of innovation because they, by nature of their integrated thinking process, can see not just the *why*, but also the *how* of bringing a vision to fruition.

The way we work today is more streamlined than the way we worked a bit earlier in the web's evolution. But, for now, hybrid personalities seem to be unfortunately rare. When I meet someone who isn't intimidated by either programming or design, it's usually someone who got started in the online industry very early. This is because most businesses structure the workflow in a way that limits employees. Giving employees a rigid job structure might make it easier to find the right person to blame when something goes wrong, but it's not conducive in the least to producing the best end product.

Of course, there are those who disagree. James Eberhardt, team lead for technology and development at Infinet Communications, says, "You let designers design, and programmers program; then each of them will perform their task at a higher level than if they had to do both. The end product will be superior."

But is that true? Not in my experience. How many times do people knock heads, make unreasonable requests, and waste each other's time with fruitless arguments that wouldn't have had to occur if they better understood the other person's position?

Savvy project managers who are interested in rapid site development and deployment can use employees' individual strengths to advance that end. In fact, project managers spend most of their time translating program limitations to designers and vice versa. This places the onus of effective team management and quality results on a single person. It's a simple model, but not an effective one. Let individuals work it out, and give them a sense of responsibility—and ultimately pride—in the combined effort.

Encouraging Multiple Interests

If there's a split between designers and programmers in the workplace, that rift can delay completion of project goals. Even if you add a good project manager to the mix, the separation means that an awareness of problems, limitations, and general concerns must be communicated through a second party.

Let's consider an imaginary case. The designer on our fictitious team is working in Photoshop, generating images for an approved composition. But the programmer has been told that certain portions of each page need to be dynamically updated. Looking at the design together, the programmer and the designer can easily solve problems that might arise before generating the graphics and code. But if they just have their individual specs and follow them, the debugging occurs after the fact—and, in some cases, that means redesigning the whole approach.

If the project had begun with everyone working together in a round-table fashion, the problem might have been avoided. What's more, when all working members of a web team educate each other about limitations, it saves a great deal of time and money.

In this scenario, the manager's role shifts from one of total responsibility to one of management and support. The manager can now focus on encouraging development of hybrid skill sets so that team members can communicate even more effectively, instead of chugging along separately and trying to cram everything together on deadline.

If the manager works to integrate employee skills and support hybrid personalities in roles most suited to them, he can create a production process that really involves teamwork and that uses each team member's talents to the utmost.

But managers often crush hybrid potential without even knowing it. This usually happens because the manager in question is unaware of an individual team member's thoughts about the production process.

If you're a project manager, it's imperative to talk to your team members and find out what each individual perceives as his unique strengths and interests. No matter the pressures and deadlines involved in web development and design, if the project manager misses these concerns, there will be a fundamental weakness in the ability of the team to integrate ideas effectively. So, think about the personalities of your team, and encourage all members to communicate their ideas without limiting themselves to a particular job designation.

Integrated Design

The scarcity of hybrid personalities is due in part to education. Add to that a workplace tendency to keep the design and technology departments separate, and problems arise with communication, in streamlining the work process, and, of course, in innovation.

But, ultimately, the choice is our own. We need to look first at why integrated thinking can be so empowering, and then we need to seek out exercises that help us strengthen those areas of weakness in a constructive, fun way.

As you read and work through this book, my hope is that it will become increasingly obvious that opening ourselves to avenues that are yet unexplored, or that are perhaps unexplored because we simply have not had the time, will give us all a great opportunity to become better integrated in general. The beauty of this integration is that it does not stop at the professional level, but it can profoundly and forever alter you as an individual in very positive, fulfilling ways.

CHAPTER 2

The Basis of Integrated Thinking on the Web

When you dive in for your morning swim, climb the stairs to wake your child, or walk to the corner store for a cold drink on a hot day, your body is responding to complex commands and impulses to get these tasks done. The human brain oversees these day-to-day activities; most of the time, we don't think about how complex the process is. A great example is driving—the process becomes rote. We don't think about it overtly, but the truth is, our brains perform complex biochemical and behavioral procedures involving learning, information processing, and memory to accomplish even the most seemingly mundane tasks.

Web designers and developers are challenged in a way that very few learners and thinkers are challenged. Not only is the complexity of the subjects that we study a concern, but the rate at which we must absorb that information and put it into practice seems unprecedented. We also have to manage the doing as well as the thinking: the hands-on creation of technology and design for web sites. All of these acts demand knowledge that is both broad and wide, and we must access that knowledge as quickly and as painlessly as going to the corner store for that cold beer.

As we seek to become more effective web designers and developers, our brains similarly must manage the complex process of learning, processing information, and rapidly storing that information into memory.

I'm of the mind-set that we can all become better at what we do by first giving ourselves credit for the interest in and fascination with a field whose very essence demands that its professionals think technologically and artistically. Then, to grow in our work, we must identify our strengths, be honest regarding our weaknesses, and push ourselves to find ways to improve our skills to achieve innovation.

Information Processing and Human Learning

Integration is necessary for the web designer and developer. This perspective arises out of the idea that most of our work is split between logic and creativity. That we must be logical and creative *at the same time* within any facet of our job reflects this split, and it is from this split that the idea of integration comes about.

But where did the idea of this split originate? A field of study known as *learning theory* focuses on this very issue. The specific theory of greatest interest to this discussion is referred to as *split brain* (see Figure 2.1). In split-brain theory, the pervasive belief is that the left and right hemispheres of the brain are each responsible for distinct types of information processing.

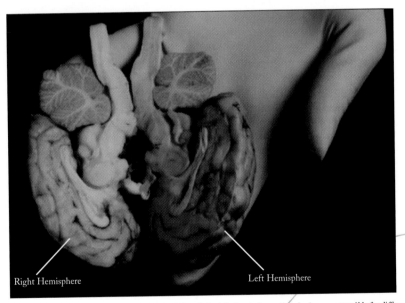

Right Hemisphere   Left Hemisphere

*Figure 2.1   Split brain theory suggests that the left and the right hemispheres of the brain are responsible for different kinds of information processing (**www.exploratorium.edu/memory/braindissection/index.html**).*

For more than 40 years, a psychobiologist named Roger Sperry studied the brain's physical functions. He found that the left side of the brain is typically more dominant, and is involved in reason and language. The right hemisphere has instead a nonverbal focus. According to this theory, it is responsible for such expressions as art, music, and other creative processes.

While split-brain theory is somewhat dated as a scientific concept, it is a very common metaphor that people use to describe themselves. Because of its common use, I use the metaphor here to help clarify the essence of the communication: That most people are not integrated in their thinking and as such require more information on how to achieve a more holistic viewpoint.

Perhaps the most intriguing part of split-brain theory is that, despite the theory's basis that certain activities are managed by independent sides of the brain, people ultimately rely on both sides—our mental processes somehow, somewhere integrate.

Most people do have specific strengths in the way they think. Some people are very adept at using their whole brain. Others have a more overt dominant hemisphere.

Roger Sperry received a Nobel Prize in 1981 for his studies, and his work is credited with having opened up new pathways of exploration in both psychology and biology.

Unlike other aspects of cognitive function, emotions have never been readily confinable to one hemisphere… emotional effects tend to spread rapidly to involve both hemispheres.

—Roger Sperry in his Nobel Lecture, 1981

Sperry points to the emotions as involving both hemispheres. It's possible to take Sperry's perspective and suggest that integration appears boldly at the emotional level. To create something new, to innovate, can be seen as some combination of left-brain logic and right-brain creativity. Add emotion, which is necessary to promote new ideas, and it's possible to suggest that mental integration is the precursor to innovation.

Of course, without the ability to express an idea in some articulate way, that idea cannot come to fruition. In order to go from integration to innovation to the *expression* of that innovation, we must have the skills and encouragement necessary to get there. True innovation involves a range of abilities, and communication becomes an essential factor when bringing ideas to light.

How to Achieve Innovation

The suggestion, then, is that if we as web designers and developers want to be innovative in our work, we must understand our areas of strength and our areas of weakness. So just how do we do this? Study Table 2.1, and write down which features you feel are your strongest. Then provide yourself with a sentence or two explaining why you believe this to be true.

Table 2.1 **Left- and Right-Brain Features**

Left Brain	Right Brain
Logical	Intuitive
Sequential	Random
Rational	Holistic
Analyzes	Synthesizes
Objective	Subjective
Parts	Wholes

This is what I came up with:

- **Logical.** Do you favor logic over intuition? Logic is my default mode. If I can't deal with something random or chaotic, I use logic as a means to work through it.

- **Rational.** Are you a rationalist or do you think holistically? Although I'm not at first glance always a rational person, I am a realist, which suggests to me that I process information in a rational way.

- **Analytical.** Do you analyze or synthesize? I have a friend who once said, "Hand Molly a plain white piece of paper, and you'll have an analysis back in less than five minutes."

- **Intuitive.** If you are intuitive, can you also be logical? Perhaps it is my gender—or just my personality—but I am very aware of my intuition and have found that when I don't listen to it, I end up hurt.

- **Holistic.** Do you find that your thinking tends to be very open minded, or more concerned with empiric evidence? Big-picture thinking suits me. I'm passionate but not always very precise. And, while I am interested in the empiric, I have never had a need to have proof of something in order to agree with its possibilities.

- **Wholes.** Do you see things in their distinct parts, or do you see whole groups? First, I see the composition, the whole. Then I see what it's made up of. I think in terms of wholes rather than parts.

Explore your personal results, and take some time to consider what they mean. This is an important exercise, because it will help you gain a better sense of how you learn, solve problems, and ultimately, how you will be best able to strengthen any weaknesses and feel confident about your strengths.

It's interesting to consider that half of my strengths come from the left brain, whereas the other half come from the right brain. Like many readers of this book, I am already integrated to some degree. But there are areas in which I am definitely weaker on both sides, and these are the areas that need attention.

Early education, at least in most high-tech societies, tends to favor left-brain modes of thinking while down-playing right-brain modes. This could be at the core of some of our real challenges: We've been educated and enculturated to think in specific ways—even if those ways are not natural to our own, unique patterns.

Human Memory as a Metaphor for the Web

While how we think individually makes an enormous impact on how well equipped we are to be innovative as web designers and developers, how our brains work physiologically also has impact on how we work with and grow the web.

The comparison of the human brain to computers is not only common-place, but it also has gained broad acceptance in psychological, philosophical, and computer science communities. Some very general comparisons include those listed in Table 2.2.

Table 2.2 Brain and Computer

Brain	Computer
Nerve cells	CPU
Long-term memory	Hard drive
Short-term memory	RAM

The web can be seen as comparable to the pathways of human memory. The best way to quickly understand this concept is through analogy.

My father died some 13 years ago. Let's say that someone in my family brings up his name. His name can act as the spark that starts my memory working. An image of my father comes to the forefront of my mind.

But the information that makes up my father's image is not stored all in one file or even in one specific part of my brain. It is, in fact, broken up into minute pieces of memory data and is strewn far and wide in various neural pockets, just as various bits of information on a web site are located in different files or directories. To put together the image of my dad, my brain has to collect all the bits of data—eyes, nose, mouth, ears, body—by rapidly traveling on a variety of neural pathways and ultimately putting them together in one cohesive piece. If these processes work, I end up with the image of my father.

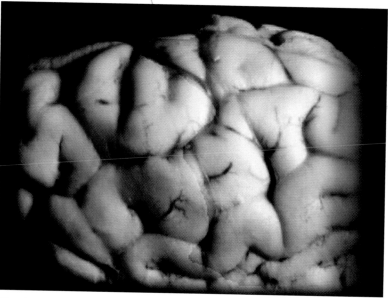

Figure 2.2   Mid-section of the brain (**www.exploratorium.edu/memory/braindissection/index.html**).

Memory, like the web, can be argued as being nonlinear. Yet typically, most westerners have learned to read left to right, we conceive time as being linear, and we usually receive information passively from a single source such as a parent, a teacher, or the TV. We also tend to process information in a linear fashion—but *only* because we've learned to do it that way.

Memory can be thought of as a nonlinear process (see Figure 2.3), comparable to the way we perceive the data retrieval and circuitry of a web site. One piece fits into the next piece and so on, but they refer back to one another, connect over others as unrelated masses of information, and run in tangents, spirals, and spheres. It is the way in which we perceive this process that creates an opportunity for endless, creative discovery in educational and human growth potential.

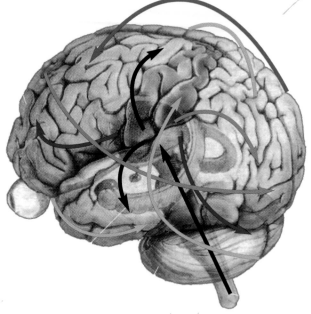

Figure 2.3 *Pathways of data traveling the brain*
(**www.exploratorium.edu/memory/braindissection/index.html**).

The experience of surfing the web is not generally a linear one (see Figure 2.4). We move through it tangentially. Our path along the way has spirals and spheres, but only sometimes do we navigate in straight lines. For these reasons, the web stands to be a potent element in the future of human development as it pertains to information absorption and processing.

The business of creating web sites challenges us to think differently than how we were taught to think. We are instead encouraged to think in the way that the facets of memory and emotion naturally exist and are expressed—complete with non sequiturs and sidebar discussions. The web is a buzz for so many people because it satisfies a very deep need to combine cerebral processes: left brain/right brain, the linear with the nonlinear, the conceptual with the concrete.

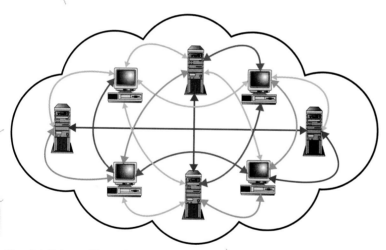

Figure 2.4 Pathways of data on the World Wide Web.

As web designers and developers, we can take the integrated potential of the web and, if we've been successful at integrating our own skills, tap into that potential as a source of inspiration. We can only benefit from understanding these interesting concepts and theories. Not only do these ideas aid us in deciding how and when to use specific approaches to a site's design, but these concepts also enable us to think about the user and his experience with the site.

Moreover, with this type of knowledge, web designers essentially plant seeds in fertile ground for high-quality communications. Even in the case of a commercial site, the opportunity for education, humor, and personal advancement exists. This is the web at its finest—a fun, informative, effective tool that has the opportunity to stimulate the mind instead of numbing it, as media which encourage passivity so often have done.

Where Integration Begins

When working on a web site, we embark on the integration of language and science, art and technology, and concept and practice the moment we create a link (hypertext) on a web page. Instead of just reading the page, our site visitors are now motivated to make a decision whether to follow that link or not. Links move us away from a static media element that encourages passivity to one that encourages activity.

Using Personal Growth to Effect Change on the Web

My stepfather is a scientist, and he pointed out to me in a conversation that evolution can be used as a terrific metaphor for the growth of the web. In the early phases of evolution, features appear and then disappear, often very quickly. At some point, the process stabilizes and the organism has a period in which some basic, shared features dominate.

But the evolutionary process is typically long. Ecosystems, for example, are old. In contrast, the web is in ridiculously nascent form. But some basic, shared features already exist in the evolution of language and science on the web.

As these shared features become more stable, we have more opportunity to determine how to help them along in their evolutionary growth. This can be clearly seen in the move toward structured markup and the use of CSS. After years of attempting to force HTML to accommodate presentational needs, we've finally realized a better approach. We could continue to try and make HTML work, but that would limit evolution.

So, we've revised our methods in accordance with the limitations we discovered. This is exactly how our own personal growth influences our work. The challenge of finding a means to visually design the web without disturbing its communicative abilities forced us to reevaluate our technical direction. This is innovation, which has in turn helped to stabilize the web's infrastructure enough so as to provide opportunities for new features to emerge. The proliferation of alternative devices and wireless access to the web exemplifies this perfectly.

Articulating the Conceptual

The interactivity that is first defined in a link and taken to new heights with imagery is exciting because its content is driven only in part by the designer. It then must be navigated by site visitors, each of whom might choose to go about the task independently. This creates an active rather than passive relationship between the user and the content. Site visitors chart their own courses through the highways and byways of a site and the other sites that it links to, depending upon the way the links appeal to them. The discovery process within this journey is the essence of new media and exemplifies nonlinear thinking. It also opens the doorways to new and exciting creations.

One of the essential elements of the web is the capability to use interactivity as a means to precisely communicate multiple thoughts, ideas, and data. A site might contain access to such documents, but within the definition of new media, content presentation demands concise expression.

In a textbook, we are allowed the liberty to explore complicated ideas within hundreds or thousands of pages. This type of exploration simply cannot occur the same way on the web, mostly due to the nature of the onscreen environment. In some instances, such as when people use commercial services for access, time online costs money, and that is a consideration as well. Web visitors often want to have their ideas delivered in a snappy, quick, and concise fashion. Many information architects and usability

Evolution, Darwin, and Innovation

These excerpts from the writing of Charles Darwin discuss evolution in a poetic, naturalistic framework. Yet the writing is scientific by influence, providing us with an excellent example of integrated thought resulting in innovation.

"The affinities of all the beings of the same class have sometimes been represented by a great tree. I believe this simile largely speaks the truth. The green and budding twigs may represent existing species; and those produced during each former year may represent the long succession of extinct species…

"The limbs divided into great branches, and these into lesser and lesser branches, were themselves once, when the tree was small, budding twigs; and this connection of the former and present buds by ramifying branches may well represent the classification of all extinct and living species in groups subordinate to groups…

"From the first growth of the tree, many a limb and branch has decayed and dropped off, and these lost branches of various sizes may represent those whole orders, families, and genera which have now no living representatives, and which are known to us only from having been found in a fossil state…

"As buds give rise by growth to fresh buds, and these, if vigorous, branch out and overtop on all a feebler branch, so by generation I believe it has been with the Tree of Life, which fills with its dead and broken branches the crust of the earth, and covers the surface with its ever branching and beautiful ramifications."

engineers suggest that ideas must be clear, written much more like headlines than detailed paragraphs. The concept is to catch the reader's eye, quickly get to the point of the site, and then offer greater details as necessary.

Interactivity can help or hinder this process, depending upon how it is used. If a hyperlink to another document is placed in the first sentence of a web site introduction, there is a chance of losing a visitor within the first several seconds of his visit. At the other extreme, if no hypermedia is used within a web document, the strengths of the web are not being exploited. It takes a strong mix of writing skills and good instinct to combine hypermedia with short, sharp language to get right to, rather than away from, the point of a site.

Ultimately, how we articulate interactivity is critical to understanding both the structure of the web and our own methods of learning, information gathering, and memory processing. In fact, the web can be seen as mimicking human memory. By understanding this, we become more intimately familiar with the structure of the web as well as our own learning processes. Take that to the next level, and you end up with the compelling idea that how we learn, integrate that learning, and express that integration is the foundation upon which truly innovative designs are built.

Integrated Design

When we compare our personal makeup and general physiology to the structure of the web, we are able to make specific, empowering connections.

Consider:

- Most education in high-tech countries tends to group us by intellectual strength rather than helping us to strengthen our less active aspects.

- How well we can integrate ideas as web designers and developers depends upon being able to strengthen our weaker aspects.

- We can use a nonlinear model of human learning and memory and compare it to the nonlinear aspects of the web, allowing us to view the web in an emotional as well as physical way.

A conclusion can be drawn, then, that the integration of our perceptions of the web with our perceptions about ourselves affords opportunities for innovation and evolution both for ourselves and for the web.

CHAPTER 3

Profiles of Integration

What experience suggests that before innovation comes integration? What anecdotes can I share to provide you with inspiration and understanding that the integration and refinement of skills relate directly to the ability of individuals to do the work of the web?

I looked to people whose work I admire to gain insight into how integration of skills has helped them perform tasks that didn't even exist 10 years ago. Not only have these individuals performed those tasks, but their contributions to the evolution and growth of the web are inarguably critical. What's more, they individually represent a range of specialties: design, development, management, and programming. What locks these individuals together is their awareness of integration and how a combination of trail-blazing ideas and nose-to-the-grindstone work can become manifest in web sites that are aesthetic and functional, that are built with visionary publishing tools, that contain vibrant online communities, and that shout out unique identities and independent voices.

No matter what the focus is, the end result is the same: One's skills must come together for that which is visionary to be first illuminated and then born

I Used to Feel Torn

Evan Williams is one of the co-founders of San Francisco–based Pyra Labs, which was formed in 1999 to build power web tools for regular people. Blogger, Pyra's first product, has been widely acknowledged as the leader of the rapidly growing weblog phenomenon, which has transformed how people—from the digerati to high school students—communicate, gather news, and share information. Today, Pyra is led practically single-handedly by Williams, who has kept Blogger alive and thriving in terms of both its technical function and its communicative reach.

Who: Evan Williams, co-creator of Blogger,
www.blogger.com; **www.evhead.com**

I used to feel torn by my artistic and technical "sides."
Growing up, I was both a "right-brained, artistic, creative
boy" and a "left-brained, logical, smart boy," but never at
the same time. Today, it's obvious to me that this division,
like so many things we're fed while growing up, is a
simplistic and false dichotomy. But when you're young,
adults often want to put you in one of society's boxes, and,
seeking to form your own identity, you want to be told
what you're good at and what you're not good at.

Perhaps never getting a clear picture of this for myself
is one of the reasons I never focused on any one area
of specialty.

All of my career skills are self-taught. Usually, they're
taught out of sheer necessity, trial and error. I get a project
in mind and simply proceed to do what is required to make
it a reality with the resources at hand. If those resources
involve other people—skilled in useful areas that I am
not—I try to take advantage and learn from those skills.
But more often (especially early on), it has been up to me
to tackle every aspect of a given situation.

That's how I became acquainted with everything from
hardware to software, pixels to programming—even
writing copy and doing the books.

Looking back, it's easy to see places where undeserved
confidence in underdeveloped skills had retrospectively
embarrassing effects. But the great thing was, I never
accepted the belief that I wasn't good at anything I tried,
and I wasn't afraid to learn anything. So, I always
got better.

This is not to say that it's better to tackle every aspect of a
project on your own or that there is not something to be
gained by spending time mastering a particular area. But
I feel that embracing both my artistic and technical skills—
and realizing that they aren't opposed to each other but
highly complementary—allows me to create more holistic
and detailed creative visions, along with a realistic sense
of how to bring them to fruition.

"I was both a 'right-brained, artistic, creative boy' and a 'left-brained, logical, smart boy' ... this division, like so many things we're fed while growing ... is a simplistic and false dichotomy."

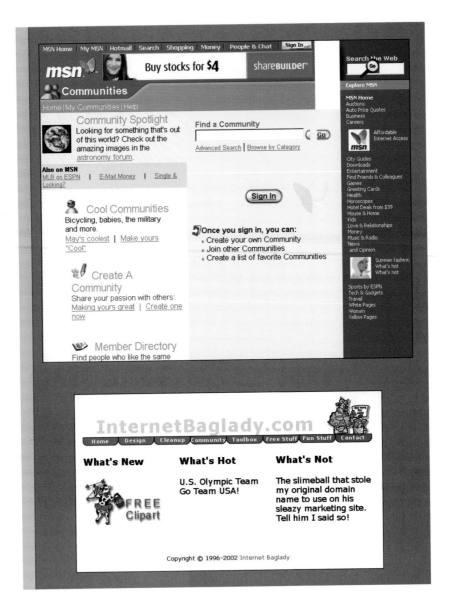

Mother of Two, Mother of Thousands

Jody McFadden has been a community category manager, community manager, chat manager, and community consultant to a multitude of online communities since 1989. She has worked for GEnie Online Services, Delphi, MSN, and the Web Review Network; she is now a consultant to companies interested in the technical creation and interpersonal management of Internet communities.

Who: Jody McFadden, online community management specialist, **www.internetbaglady.com**

It has been said that my arrival on the community scene in 1989 was via covered wagon. Remember that, in the olden days before the web, logging onto an online service was not free: Each member paid $6 an hour, and we were logging on with 1200-baud modems!

My first stop was a text-based community on GEnie Online Services. The community was focused on hobbies, and my personal interest was quilting. My first impression of the area was that it had fantastic potential but greatly lacked vision and administrative awareness of member needs. The community had terrific members yet had a manager who was an absentee landlord, at best.

Not willing to accept this situation, I decided to write the manager and list the items that our section needed to thrive. Instead of creating these items or performing the functions himself, he hired me as a category manager. Par for the course!

So there I was, a housewife and ex-nurse with no technical skills and an immediate need to know. I spent every waking hour learning the system and the software until I was able to re-create the technology *and* address usability needs.

As I went on to manage and build the community there, and beyond to MSN and the unique challenges of the web community, the integrated skills that I put on the table included a sense of humor, a vision for the future, keen observation, the ability to stimulate member interaction, patience, a thick skin, fairness in administrative decisions, and, above all, consistency.

The advice I would give to anyone who wants to become a community manager is to make sure that he or she is willing to do the following:

- Have time to devote to the day-to-day tasks
- Keep up with the latest industry information and trends regarding the subject area
- Have a genuine liking of the human race
- Make hard and consistent decisions, even if those decisions involve friends

My role as a mother and my training as a nurse helped me immensely as a community manager. Nurses are trained in the tools of observance and develop a keen sense of what a patient's needs are. The same holds true for a community manager: You must be able to observe the situation with neutral vision and find solutions that fit the needs of the majority of the community.

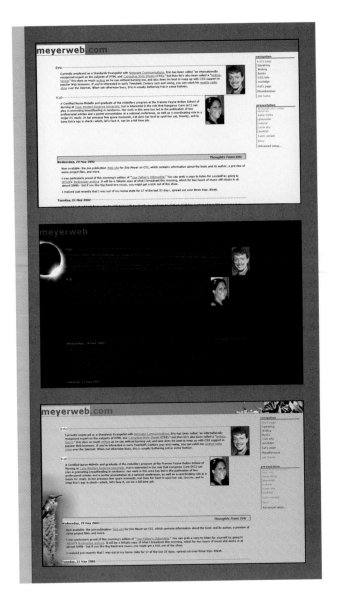

Tiny Details, Raw Mechanics

Currently employed as a standards evangelist with Netscape Communications, Eric A. Meyer has been called an internationally recognized expert on the subjects of HTML and Cascading Style Sheets (CSS), and he knows a thing or two about other aspects of web design as well. Eric does as much writing as he can without burning out, and he also does his best to keep up with CSS support in popular web browsers.

Who: Eric A. Meyer, CSS visionary and standards evangelist, **www.meyerweb.com**

The web design field is like any other: To be truly great, you have to understand the tiny details, the raw mechanics that will underlie any creation.

Dale Chihuly (**http://www.chihuly.com/**) creates incredible glass sculptures, some weighing literally tons. He can do that because he knows how glass is sculpted and fired, what its characteristics are, how to marry it to steel, and how it can be used and how it can't. And I suspect that he's always trying to figure out how to use glass in ways that even he would have thought impossible. There are thousands of scientists who understand the properties of glass as well or better, and there are thousands of artists with as much creative spirit and vision as Mr. Chihuly. But none of them does the same incredible things he does.

Other people could acquire the same skills and mimic him, of course, but that's not the point. The point is that there are thousands of glass sculptors in the world. One thing unites them: an understanding of glass and its properties. That's the technical side. What they do with that knowledge, where they take their understanding—that's the creative side. They're all using the same medium, but in what are often very different ways. Plenty of people know HTML. Every one of them does something different with it.

I don't know about other people, but sometimes I find myself analyzing real-world things—billboards, menus, magazine articles, cereal boxes, newspapers—and asking myself how I would re-create them on the web. When I'm doing that, there are two tracks in my head.

The first one is picking apart the structure, figuring out how the information relates to itself and its medium, and determining what the overall message is; the other is looking at spatial relations, color choices, curves and separators, that kind of thing. It's like there are two layers to the whole, and how they fit together and combine makes that whole what it is. Being able to see the two layers isn't unusual, but I suspect that being able to hold them both in one's head at the same time is not an ordinary thing. I also believe that it's a skill anyone can develop, with enough practice.

I'm not sure where I learned this ability, but I know that it has served me very well. There have been times when I've realized that a web design could be constructed just so, in a way that was utterly new to me. There's an indescribable feeling at those moments, when you realize that you could be the first person ever to arrive at that place. And then you feel it again, when you see it there on the screen just as you imagined it and when you think that you might well be the first person in the world to see what you're seeing, the only person to know what you now know. Nothing can top that feeling. But the odds of my having felt it would be nearly zero if I didn't have the technical know-how to realize what's possible in web design and the creative side that's always looking for new things to try.

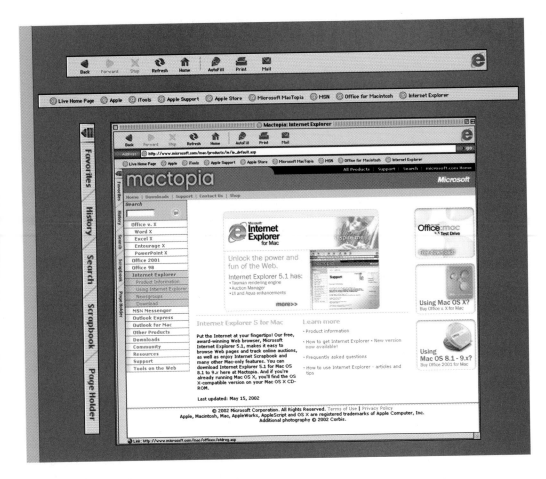

I Write Code

Tantek Çelik is a developer for Microsoft's Macintosh Internet Products Unit. As the lead developer for Macintosh Internet Explorer 5.0, his influence and concern for web standards placed the resulting browser first in line for near-complete CSS and standards support. But not only was IE 5.0 for Mac revolutionary in terms of technology; its aesthetic design has been much lauded as well. This, in turn, has influenced the inclusion of standards and improvement of user-friendliness in all contemporary web browsers.

Who: Tantek Celik, lead developer, Internet Explorer for Macintosh, **www.tantek.com**

I write code.

I have been programming since grade school. In college, I majored in computer science and subsequently completed a Master of Science degree focused on software theory. In 1997, I joined Microsoft's Macintosh Internet Products Unit and was assigned the task of implementing CSS support in Macintosh Internet Explorer. Shortly thereafter, I found out that "CSS" stood for Cascading Style Sheets.

As with many things, one must first realize the absence of understanding before understanding can be achieved. Aside from some academic and industry experience with user interface design, I had no experience with style sheets, graphical layout, typography, or any of the other concerns that CSS addresses. I immersed myself in the few CSS books that had been written at the time and numerous other texts in related areas. I surrounded myself, usually via online relationships, with experts in the field and challenged them to explain themselves.

I think that understanding might be possible. Yet other limitations—in my own ability, in time—cannot necessarily be overcome. This brings on a sense of self-humility— the realization and acceptance of one's limitations—and is critical to distinguishing that which is practical and necessary from that which is academic and unnecessary.

Such humility as applied to building a browser might lead one to conclude that rewriting everything from scratch is too difficult of an undertaking to successfully complete in a predictable amount of time. Or one might conclude that fully supporting every web standard is too big of an undertaking.

Such humility instead leads one to build upon others' work: to tweak some code instead of reworking it, to rework instead of rewriting, to rewrite in place instead of rewriting entirely from scratch, and to support a few web standards well rather than consuming more alphabet soup than one can digest.

One cannot omit the fire of creativity. There must be innovation. Creativity, above all, dictates how fast a process improves a product—or whether there is any improvement at all.

Most of CSS1 was fairly straightforward to implement. Yet a few key bits here and there required considerable creativity to properly implement.

Writing a breakthrough browser is not just a simple matter of programming. It requires that one simultaneously understand one's own abilities and limitations, that one be willing to learn new disciplines and rely on new experts. It requires bravery to attempt the unattained and the humility to keep to practical means and goals.

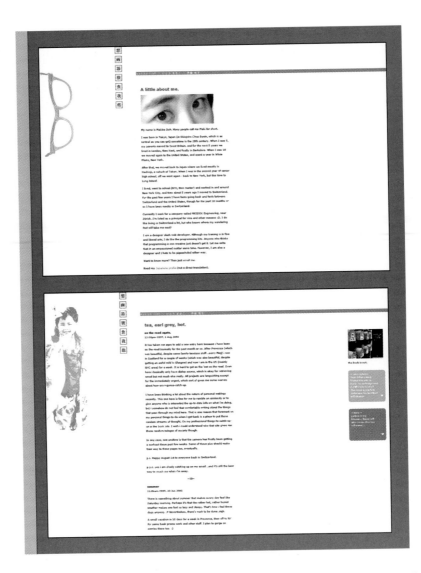

Programming Is Creative

Makiko Itoh was born in Tokyo, Japan. She has lived on and off in Japan and the United States, and she is currently living in Zurich, Switzerland. There, she works as a principal for the development company PRODOK Engineering as a designer and web developer.

Who: Makiko Itoh, PRODOK Engineering,
www.prodok.com; **www.makikoitoh.com**

Integration of skills is vital to what I do. My education and formal training are not in programming. In college, I was a fine arts and art history major. Before I entered the web creation field, I worked as a graphic designer and art director at an ad agency. However, I have always been interested in computers and programming.

One thing that has given me an advantage has been the fact that computers don't intimidate me. Programming doesn't intimidate me. To me, computers and programs are merely another tool. To get the most of out of the tools, you have to become proficient at using them.

Take Photoshop. Sure, you can get by just scratching the surface of the program, relying on plug-ins and predefined actions. But if you learn more about how the program actually works in a technical sense, then creative possibilities increase exponentially.

The same goes with the skills involved in web page creation. The code that makes up a web page—the markup, styles, and scripts, both client-side and server-side—are all there to create the final product. That product is the web: a largely *visual* means of communication. Because I want to explore the possibilities offered by the different tools and languages available for creating the web, I try, at the minimum, to understand what each tool does. Every time I can add a tool to my toolbox, my range increases.

Currently, my actual work is a lot more technical and developmental than visual design–related. This is due to the nature of the projects that my company receives from clients. But I believe that my background in design gives me an advantage. I know how designers think and what they expect, so it's easier for me to both translate their requests to code and communicate technical knowledge to them.

Visual training is perhaps harder to acquire than technical training. But if you are dealing with a visual medium, getting that training is totally necessary. I think that you can gain a lot more by getting formal design training. Programming and technical training can, with some perseverance and success, be studied on one's own.

Programming can be creative. It could be more like creating music than painting a picture, but nevertheless it is a lot of fun. Orchestrating a web site or an electronic workflow is much more involved than creating a pretty interface, and in many ways the stuff you don't see—the logic—is much more fun and creative.

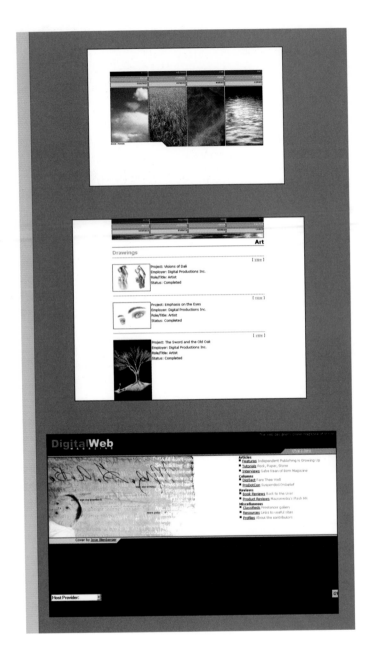

The Independent Web: Nick Finck

Nick Finck is the editor in chief of *Digital Web Magazine*. He is a freelance web designer in Portland, Oregon, and he spends most of his copious free time snowboarding the slopes of the Cascade Mountains.

Who: Nick Finck, editor in chief of *Digital Web Magazine,* **www.digital-web.com**; **www.nickfinck.com**

When I built my first web page in 1994, I never imagined the breadth of skills that would be required to build a complete site from scratch just a few years later. Neither did I imagine what I would be able to create with those skills. For me, nothing happened overnight. It took years to come to the realization of what I really wanted to create and how I was going to go about creating it.

My first web site was hideous, but I wasn't alone. In the mid- to late 1990s, everyone had poorly designed static sites because everyone was taking their first stab at the technology. The same technology still exists today, but it came of age—or at least grew in complexity. There is no longer a set of markup "takes" that could be written within the confines of a single sheet of paper. Now it seems that markup for a site would require hundreds of pages for its documentation.

As technology improves, it rarely keeps its simplicity. You no longer design a web site according to the specific amount of content on it. Today the content changes; it's dynamically driven from databases, and you must create designs and interfaces that compensate for changing amounts of content. To do this, you must have a firm understanding of both the creative and the technical aspects of web design. You must know how to make a design that is flexible and robust enough to endure the changing content—and even the possibility of the underlying technologies changing all together.

Not many people out there who I can think of have a firm understanding of both the creative and the technical aspects of web design.

Those who I can think of are quite successful, not because they are "jacks of all trades" but because they know what it takes to build a functional web site that is well-implemented and attractive to the user. I was very fortunate to have a few good mentors along the way who helped me see a better way of doing things. I believe that *Digital Web Magazine* is a direct result of understanding how the artistic and creative aspects of web design interface with the complex technical aspects of web development and web programming.

PART II

Integration Primer for the Programmatically Inclined

CHAPTER 4

Exploring Color

Pick a color, any color. Then answer these questions:

- What color did you pick?

- Is the color your favorite color?

- Is the color something you are wearing right now?

- Look around at where you're sitting. Is the color there in your environment?

- How does this color make you feel?

Color can be a very powerful and convincing means of grabbing attention and conveying emotion without ever using words. But where does color come from? And how is it perceived? Here, you'll learn the scientific basis of color, how color is perceived, and how that color can, in turn, persuade and guide people.

When you begin to study color, you should be aware of two important subtopics:

- The nature of light

- The interpretation of that light as the perception of color

Light is electromagnetic radiation. In physics, there is no difference between visible light and other forms of electromagnetic radiation, such as radio waves, microwaves, or X-rays, except that *visible* light appears within the wavelengths we can see.

The Nature of Color

Light is a form of energy. This energy, in the context of color, can be considered to have these characteristics:

- **Luminous.** It gives off light.

- **Absorbed.** Pigments absorb light; what is reflected is what is perceived.

- **Structured.** Color can come about as a result of the physical structure of an object. A duck's head appears shiny green not because of pigment but because the microstructure of the feathers is the same wavelength as the wavelength of green light.

The healthy human eye is sensitive to light that has a wavelength of between 400 and 700 nanometers (nm). A nanometer is a billionth of a meter; light travels at about one foot per nanosecond.

When an object is hot, it gives off some of its energy as electromagnetic radiation. In simple terms, this can be thought of as *luminosity*—the emission of light. When you pop your morning toast into the toaster and it begins to heat up—but not enough for the heating elements to glow yet—it gives off heat in the form of infrared radiation. The human eye just can't see that radiation (unless the owner of that eye happens to have a military scope that's sensitive to infrared).

But as the toaster gets hotter, the wavelength of the radiation that it gives off gets shorter and the element begins to glow red—and this we can easily see. In fact, the wavelength corresponding to red is the longest wavelength of light that we are capable of seeing (see Figure 4.1).

As the heating element gets even hotter, the wavelength becomes shorter and the light given out contains all the colors of the visible spectrum. When this happens, we no longer see red, but we see white (see Figure 4.2). This concept has even worked its way into our vocabulary and popular culture.

> *While color can accurately be measured at its source, the perception of color is subjective.*

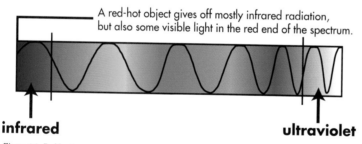

A red-hot object gives off mostly infrared radiation, but also some visible light in the red end of the spectrum.

infrared

ultraviolet

Figure 4.1 Red heat.

"White Heat, Red Hot"

—Judas Priest, 1978

"The father's son, thy kingdom come, electric ecstasy.

"Deliver us from all the fuss and give us sanctuary.
Lead us all into arena, magnificent in death.
Well let us serenade the sinner, we'll follow in his step.

"White heat, red hot burns deep, white heat red hot.

"The fury songs, venomous wrongs so rich in tragedy,
An overture forever more to senseless victories.
Give to us this day of glory the power and the kill
So we avoid the wrath and all the almighty fire of

"White heat, red hot burns deep, white heat red hot.
The heat's hot burns a lot.
Who are not cut out to fight this day will surely fall.
The few who stand to take command forever and ever
* are men.*

"Prepare to fight, unsheathe your scythe a ghastly beam of ill
To slice the life with blinding light and seventh–
* dimensional skill.*

"The centuries of dedication inherited till at last
From years of solar gladiation can only end in

"White heat, red hot burns deep, white heat red hot.
The heat's hot burns a lot.
Who are not cut out to fight this day will surely fall.
The few who stand to take command forever and ever
* are men."*

White heat
Red hot
White heat
Red hot.

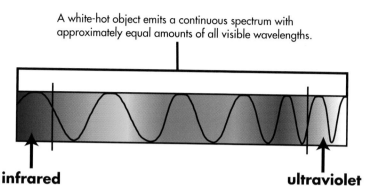

A white-hot object emits a continuous spectrum with approximately equal amounts of all visible wavelengths.

infrared   **ultraviolet**

Figure 4.2 White heat.

Just the other day I went into the store to buy light bulbs. It had been a while since I'd purchased light bulbs, so I was kind of surprised to see the variety of bulbs now available for standard use. There are common incandescent bulbs, fluorescent bulbs, full-spectrum bulbs, and more. And all of these bulbs come in different, albeit subtle, color ranges.

Light bulbs—and objects in general—give off light not only when they are hot, but also any time atoms are active. A fluorescent light bulb is not necessarily hot, but the atoms within it are active. Therefore, light (and color) results.

Pick a Color

This exercise provides the opportunity to notice how colors are used in everyday life. Remember the color that you picked at the beginning of this chapter? Put this book aside for a bit, get away from the computer, and call your dog, your spouse, or a willing child. Go outside for a walk and look around you for the color you picked.

What objects are that color? Is the color hot? Cool? How many variations can you find in nature or via human hands? What does the color make you feel? Do variations of the color make you feel differently?

The scientific-minded among you might be tempted to take notes as you walk. But the critical point is to just take notice of where and how your color appears, what it makes you think of, and what it makes you feel.

When you get back inside, write down your thoughts. Then open your favorite imaging program—say, Photoshop or Illustrator, and create a visual design of any kind (logo, web page mockup, free-form artistic meanderings) using only your chosen color and variations on that color.

Using one color and its variants in design is referred to as a monochromatic palette (Figure 4.3).

*Figure 4.3   The "Pick a Color" exercise results in a monochromatic palette. In Photoshop,
I opened a digital photo I'd taken in the famous Lafayette Cemetery in
New Orleans, desaturated it, and applied a single color. Then I adjusted
the contrast and brightness to bring out more of the color's variations.*

Absorption is the most common phenomenon that gives an object color. When light hits the object, not all of the wavelengths of light are reflected equally.

Suppose that a continuous spectrum of somewhat red light hits an object. Also suppose that the object in question absorbs more of the light from the red end of the spectrum. The spectrum of light reflected from the object will be graphed in an irregular pattern of light of different wavelengths.

The Perception and Processing of Color

Perception is inherently subjective. What I perceive and what you perceive will never be exactly the same. There are numerous reasons for this. First, we don't possess the same physical attributes. In terms of vision, our eyes are physically different—I have very good vision but am also farsighted. As a result, my eyes tire easily and I tend to be more photosensitive than others. You might be nearsighted or color blind. Others might have more serious problems with their vision—or might even have no vision whatsoever.

The World Health Organization (WHO) estimates that approximately 38 million people worldwide are blind and that more than 110 million have low vision. This is roughly an overall blindness rate of 7 people per 1,000.

We also perceive color with sociological and psychological influences. Culture often determines someone's archetypal response to a color, and our individual psyches also respond to color in a very personal way (see Table 4.1). My childhood bedroom was pink and green. In my upbringing, those colors were feminine, young, warm, and spirited.

Diffraction and Refraction

Light waves that pass the surface or edges of a single object are bent as a result. This is referred to as diffraction.

Diffraction produces a fuzzy area between what is light and what is shadow. Because of the wave nature of light, the waves are superimposed; as a result, different colors travel in different directions. Therefore, when you look at a CD, you see a rainbow of different colors.

Light travels with greater speed through different objects. Let's say that light is moving through the air and into my beer glass. The light moves more quickly through the air. But if the light wave hits my beer glass at an angle, that light wave will be split—one side of the wave will continue to change direction when it enters the glass in which it travels more slowly than in air, resulting in refraction. The waves are bent as a result of interacting with more than one object, each of a different optical density.

What colors do you remember from the rooms of your childhood? Can you think of any personal, cultural, or family values that have given you a specific relationship to a given color? Note that color meanings are often paradoxical. It's up to you to choose a palette that works to the advantage of a given design.

Table 4.1 Color Meanings and Perceptions Around the World

Color	Psychological Response	Notes of Interest
Red	Power, energy, warmth, passion, love, aggression, danger	Changes meaning in the presence of other colors. With green, it becomes a symbol of Christmas. When combined with white, it means joy in many eastern cultures.
Blue	Trust, conservatism, security, technology, cleanliness, order	Used in the United States by many banks to symbolize trust.
Green	Nature, health, good luck, jealousy ("green with envy"), renewal	Doesn't do well in a global market. Problems are associated with green packaging in China and France. Green has been successful in attracting investors in the Middle East, however.
Yellow	Optimism, hope, philosophy, dishonesty, cowardice (a coward can be described as "yellow"), betrayal	Is a sacred color to Hindus.
Purple	Spirituality, mystery, royalty, transformation, cruelty, arrogance	Appears very rarely in nature.
Orange	Energy, balance, warmth	Signifies that a product is inexpensive (in the United States, and outside of Halloween and St. Patrick's Day).

Color	Psychological Response	Notes of Interest
Brown	Earth, reliability, comfort, endurance	Often appears on food packaging in the United States. In Colombia, brown discourages sales.
Gray	Intellect, futurism, modesty, sadness, decay	Considered to be one of the easiest colors for the eye to physically see. It is also restful to the eye.
White	Purity, cleanliness, precision, innocence, sterility, death	Signifies marriage in the United States but represents death in India and other eastern cultures.
Black	Power, sexuality, sophistication, death, mystery, fear, unhappiness, elegance	Signifies death and mourning in many western cultures. In packaging, conveys elegance, wealth, and sophistication.

To get some help on and insight into how complexities of color can be tamed by web designers seeking to create strong relationships with their site visitors, I turned to Jill Morton, an author, designer, and professor at the University of Hawaii. Morton is considered one of few world experts on color, and she has done studies regarding color in advertising design and on the web. Her work offers some wonderful insights into color and how to use it in a global environment:

- Begin with your audience. Know your target market and adjust accordingly.

- Blue is the most globally accessible color. It's safe in almost every culture. As a result, you can use blue (and hues of blue) in almost any kind of site, regardless of its audience, goal, or location.

Seeing What's Not There

The colors that we physically see are close to the spectrum of light. But we can also see colors that are not found in the spectrum.

This happens when wavelengths near the two ends of the visible spectrum hit our retinas.

Our brains connect these wavelengths, these two "ends" of the visual spectrum, and create a figurative circle. We then "see" colors such as purple and magenta.

- Become aware of the subtleties of international perception. Pink is a great example. In East India, pale pink is considered feminine, so you would not want to use it very boldly on a site that caters to men. But in other countries, such as Japan, pastels are very popular with both men and women.

- The most unsafe color in the global environment is purple. In Catholic Europe, purple symbolizes death and crucifixion. In fact, during Victorian times, purple and its hues (lavender, for example) were used as often as black to represent mourning. In the contemporary U.S., purple is used as a symbol of lesbian feminist pride. Purple is also symbolic of mystical and unconventional spiritual beliefs that go against Christian, Jewish, and Muslim paradigms.

A case in point that I refer to in most of my writings about color is the launch of Euro Disney. The first design for signs used large amounts of purple, which visitors found "morbid." This response was completely contradictory to the happy message that Disney wanted to convey. As a result, Disney had to rework its European advertising campaign, which doubtlessly wound up costing significant money and time.

So, when discussing color from a perceptual, abstract basis, color is nearly impossible to pin down. This is one of the reasons that there are so many discrepancies in color names, individual perceptions of color, and the significance of color in a social context. What's more, the theories that have evolved over time to help us reproduce color in print or onscreen are often limited and confusing.

Subtractive Synthesis

The traditional color wheel, which you might remember from elementary school, describes primary colors—red, blue, and yellow—and the secondary colors of purple, green, and orange (see Figure 4.4).

This color wheel represents the color theory referred to as *subtractive synthesis*. Subtractive synthesis describes a theory of color in which the following are true:

- Light is absorbed by pigment (hence, *subtractive*).

- The light that is reflected by that pigment creates our perception of color.

- Color has primary, secondary, and tertiary structures, as well as a variety of other potential combinations, resulting in a spectrum of known and perceived colors.

As any print designer knows, color printing has been around for more than a century and has developed a very precise method of reproducing just about any color.

The traditional concept of primary colors as described by subtractive synthesis proved limiting in the context of print, which mixes inks and pigments to produce color. A new color ideology emerged, using cyan, yellow, and magenta (CMY) as the primary colors. Black is added (CMYK) to overcome the effect of impurities in CMY pigment that prevent those colors, when combined, from creating a true black. Figure 4.5 shows the CMYK wheel.

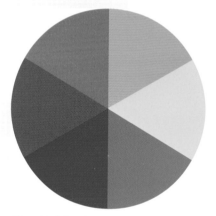

Figure 4.4 Subtractive synthesis: The familiar color wheel based on primary and secondary colors.

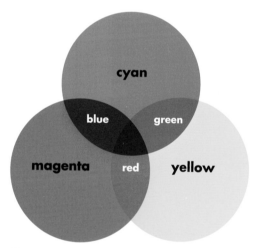

Figure 4.5 Cyan, magenta, yellow, black: A corrected color wheel for printing.

Paint Store

Red can generate excitement or arouse anger. Yellow is typically used to grab attention—with yield signs, for example.

Take a trip to a paint store and check out the different samples on display. Which ones grab your attention? Which are pleasing to you? Which are not? Which are fun? Professional? Which make you hungry? Tired?

Take home as many paint samples as you can. Cut them up and make a collage with the colors that attract you. Don't think about trying to make the colors purposely look good together—just open up your intuitive, creative self and combine the colors that feel good.

Additive Synthesis

Another color theory is *additive synthesis*. This theory applies to the screen: computer monitors and televisions. In this case, the idea is that there are three primary colors: red, green, and blue (RGB). To get white, you add (hence, *additive*) the three colors together. This produces the entire range of color, which we perceive as white (see Figure 4.6).

Secondary colors in additive synthesis are magenta, yellow, and cyan (notice that these are the primary colors in subtractive synthesis for print). If you remove all additive colors, you end up with the absence of color, which is what we perceive as black.

Using combinations of red, green, and blue, it is possible to reproduce any color. This is somewhat different than the subtractive process, which requires black in CMYK printing to reproduce certain hues, values, and saturations of that color.

You Are Blue

One morning before work, pick a color and write a few sentences describing you, the color, in the first person:

"I am blue—cool, smooth, the color of the ocean near Hawaii and off the coast of Florida on a bright sunny day."

Then, just for fun, wear that color all day.

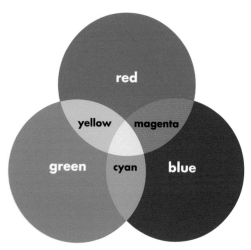

Figure 4.6 RGB color wheel, with primary and secondary colors.

Color is problematic for several reasons, beginning with the issue of perception. Scientifically, there are difficulties with color reproduction as well.

Ever notice how you *thought* your clothes matched? When you got dressed this morning in the fluorescent lighting in the bathroom, the colors sure looked fine together. Then, when you got out into the sunlight, you discovered that your colors not only didn't match, but they possibly even clashed!

As you already are aware, color is very difficult to re-create consistently on the computer screen. This is one reason we have the web-safe palette, which, of course, really isn't safe at all but does provide slightly more stability in terms of reproducing color.

Where do these troubles come from, and can they be corrected? Well, begin by assuming that there is such a thing as perfect white light. This light has exactly the same intensity for all wavelengths within the spectrum. Place a green object in the light, and it will absorb most of the two ends of the spectrum and reflect a variety of wavelengths, from spectral yellow to spectral blue, which will be perceived by the healthy eye as blue-green.

Color Quandaries

If we put the same green object in an imperfect white light, we'll get different results because of the different intensities of wavelengths. As a result, our object will be perceived as being a different color.

My stepfather tells an interesting story relating to color. He was on a trip and had rented a red car. He parked it in a restaurant parking lot and went in to have dinner. When he returned to the parking space, his car appeared white rather than red because the parking lot had turned on numerous fluorescent lights that emit a red color. Because the red car reflected all of the light that hit it, it *appeared* to be the same color as the white objects around it.

Computer screen technology has not had the time to develop as much as print technology. If all computer screens and TVs used the same phosphors or other systems to produce red, green, and blue (RGB), more consistency could be achieved. But there's not been a lot of incentive to produce more consistent colors. Think of television—if flesh tones on your TV are reasonably close to normal, you're going to be pretty accepting of that.

So, although the technology does exist or can be developed to get us closer to consistent screen color, not a lot of drive has gone into improving the situation. As a result, anyone developing and designing for the screen must have at least a basic understanding of the limitations of color technologies to better serve organizations or clients.

Coloring Book

Creativity can come from recalling how we were as kids. You can still put yourself into that mind-set by doing some of the things you enjoyed back then. Coloring is a fun way to do this (and it's cheaper than therapy or hypnosis). Just pick up a coloring book and some crayons, and go to it.

But there's one hitch. After you finish a picture, look at your color choices. Did you go for all the logical colors—green for plants, yellow for the sun? Why? What could you have done differently?

Helpful URLs

Introduction to Color: Color 101
www.webdesignclinic.com/ezine/v1i1/color/

Color Matters
www.colormatters.com

Color Voodoo
www.colorvoodoo.com

"The Meaning of Color for Gender,"
by Natalia Khouw
www.colormatters.com/khouw.html

Subtractive color synthesis
www.bway.net/~jscruggs/sub.html

Additive color synthesis
www.bway.net/~jscruggs/add.html

Integrated Design

So how do you, as a web developer, integrate the scientific and aesthetic issues related to color? Here are some ideas:

- Understand that print and screen colors are created via a different process. Print color is achieved using *subtractive synthesis*, and screen colors are produced using *additive synthesis*.

- Keep in mind that although there is a scientific basis for color, color is *perceived*. As a result, you'll want to make decisions about using color based on your audience (see Table 4.2).

- Gender has an influence on the way colors are perceived, so the audience again comes into play (see Table 4.2).

- Culture has a profound influence on color (see Table 4.2).

Table 4.2 Designing for Special Audience Needs

Audience	Color Concern	Best Practice
Men and women 40 years and older.	Low vision and aging vision affect color perception.	Use high-contrast colors (such as black on white) for this audience.
Predominantly male audience— any age, all cultures.	One in every 12 males has some problem with color perception, and 1 in every 20 men has actual color blindness. Although women also suffer from color blindness, the prevalence is much lower. As a result, predominantly male audiences would indicate a need to design for color blindness.	Avoid the use of red, green, brown, gray, or purple in your designs, and especially avoid trying to place these colors next to one another. To distinguish items very clearly, use yellow, blue, white or black, and use high contrast between foreground and background. Do not rely on color alone to draw attention to important content.
Predominantly women— any age, all cultures.	Color perception in gender is not that well studied, but academic research into the field has shown that men and women perceive color quite differently.	Use red instead of blue because red stands out more than blue to women. Women typically respond to yellow very positively but respond to orange less so. Of the two, men prefer orange. In general, women's color tastes are more diverse than men's, so you can use a wider range or variety of colors when designing for audiences that are predominantly female.
Localized audience (strong cultural influences, such as for a site that will be frequented by a particular cultural or religious sect).	Cultural perceptions of color will influence the perceived meaning of a given design.	Use colors appropriate for that culture's belief system.
Global audience (people of all ages, cultural backgrounds, and vision types).	A variety of physical and perceptual concerns arise in mixed, global audiences.	Follow good general practices, avoid problem colors (such as purple), and use good foreground/background contrast to ensure readability.

CHAPTER 5

Making Space

Space is the absence of some *thing*. That thing can be text, images, animation—any component on a web page that renders visually can be seen as antispace.

It might surprise you that our work will either fail or succeed based on how well we create space on our pages.

Space is necessary for several very important reasons:

- Proper use of space can physically guide the eye to a point on a page that is of primary interest.

- Space cushions text and images, allowing the eyes to rest. Reading onscreen is hard enough on the eyes; providing enough whitespace means improving readability (and, therefore, comprehension) of the content.

- Our brains need a break, too! Processing lots of visual information means having to concentrate. Space gives us time to process information intellectually. As with vision, the correct application of visual space results in a site visitor's better comprehension of the information presented.

Space also has some curious psychosocial implications:

- How much physical space (such as land or the size of our home) we own often reflects our individual economic strength or weakness. Designers who effectively use space can communicate a sense of sophistication and privilege or a casual and relaxed environment to match their audience's needs and web site goals.

- People need a certain amount of emotional space (hence the lover's cry, "Give me my space!"). So, space is not just absence of physical components, but it is a psychological feeling as well. If you want your audience to experience a high-energy, dynamic event, space can be minimized to compress a site visitor's emotions. If you want to help a visitor feel relaxed, use broader expanses of space between objects.

- People also need physical space. The need for this space is determined by the individual as well as his or her culture. Some people just don't like to get too physically close to others. Sometimes this is the result of emotional trauma or abuse; sometimes it's just a personal preference. Providing sufficient visual space helps people not only to relax, but focus more efficiently on content.

> *Culturally, the amount of physical space needed by a person is often seen in how people stand in groups. In the United States, people in a group normally stand with about 12–18 inches of distance between each person. In Latin American countries, people in a group tend to stand significantly closer.*

Giving a man space is like giving a dog a computer: the chances are, he will not use it wisely.

—Bette-Jane Raphael

So how does all of this relate to what happens when you sit down to create a design for the computer screen? Consider that screen space is limited. Most people do not have 21-inch monitors with which to view your site. As a result, space on the computer is prized. If we take Robertson's ideas about space to heart (see the sidebar "When Less Is More"), we find that the small amount of visual real estate on the screen demands that a refined, sophisticated, and privileged design will have plenty of space.

Space provides visual and intellectual breathing room. Space gives our eyes a comfortable place to rest, helps guide our eyes to focus on important items, and makes information processing easier. But whether the reasons are physical, emotional, cultural, or economic, the bottom line is that space must be used effectively. Space ultimately leads us to that crucial moment when we pause, absorb, and effectively process the content that is before us.

Space Invaders

I have often told this story about the New York apartments of my childhood, but it's such a great analogy that I keep returning to it. Perhaps you'll relate to in some way.

My relatives settled all around Brooklyn, New York, in apartments with small, city-style rooms. Typically, they had jammed into those rooms every heavy piece of furniture brought over from the old country. On sideboards were lace doilies, silver serving dishes, candlesticks, and other family heirlooms. Coffee tables and side tables were covered with knickknacks, bric-a-brac, collectible this, and sentimental that.

At the rowdy young age of 4, I always felt tense and awkward in this environment. I couldn't move around; it seemed as though I would literally suffocate in the clutter. It wasn't that my relatives weren't clean—goodness knows, you could eat off of their floors (so they always said!), but they just had so much jammed into an already small space.

Without space, a web page runs the risk of being like one of these apartments, making your site visitors feel tense and cluttered. On a web page, this would be heavy, unbalanced graphics competing with text that is too large or too small; the placement of objects too close to one another; and the placement of too many objects— especially ones that blink, move, or distract the eye.

When Less Is More

Print designer Keith Robertson wrote an essay for a simply fantastic book called **Looking Closer: Critical Writings on Graphic Design** *(New York: Allworth Press, 1994). In his essay, "On White Space: When Less Is More," Robertson poses an idea about why space is so culturally important.*

"White space," he writes, "is extravagance. White space is the surface of the paper on which you are printing showing through and on which you are choosing not to print."

In a tighter economy, he explains, the designer will use as much space on a page as possible. But if prosperity reigns, wasting space is a sign of privilege.

Part of your job when creating web pages is to keep your pages light and simple wherever possible. This doesn't mean that you have to restrict yourself, but you should place each component on a page with a purpose in mind.

If you have a tiny room with no windows, how do you make it look bigger? For one thing, you can paint it white or another light color. You can also remove all the heavy furnishings and tchotchkes, and furnish the room with easy, clean pieces made up of glass or metal—all lines and no clutter. In a similar vein, when a designer focuses on function, such as facilitating communication and navigation via space and position of objects that do not disrupt but rather guide the visual process, the experience becomes a much richer one for site audiences.

Similarly, when seeking to lighten up a web page, several technical issues can assist you in resolving aesthetic ones. Here are a few general ideas when creating space:

- Be aware of your visitors' screen resolutions and viewing preferences.

- Avoid, wherever possible, adding elements that aren't necessary to the page's content. There will be instances, such as with ads, where you might not be able to design to your best abilities. But, if you keep the entire visual space in mind, you'll be able to better balance your content with any additional content you might have to include on your page.

- Balance the size and weight of page elements as per the functional requirements of the page, but always keep an eye on how space and those elements are weighted.

- Make sure there's a balance of whitespace between text and images. Think of the way newspapers manage text columns and images. If text is too close to an image, it is disconcerting to the eye. Similarly, if the text is too far away, the reader will lose the contextual relationship between image and text.

- Use visual containers such as boxes and columnar data in a balanced, appropriately weighted fashion. The goal is to contain data effectively and use space to separate that data into comfortable, easily followed sections.

In the next sections, I'll explain more about each of these concerns. As your pages lighten up, your web visitors won't feel as I did in those cramped rooms—tense and out of place. Instead, they'll want to sit down and stay a while.

Coffee House

Take a trip to your local coffee house—think of it as an excuse to take a coffee break! Focus a critical eye on the access to items within the space. As you enter and walk around, notice how the store is set up. Where are the lids? The napkins? Where are there counters? Tables? Where does the line wind as it forms?

It might seem odd, but the layout of a web page is actually very much like entering a store and moving from section to section. Elements are laid out on the page for optimum usage and accessibility—or, they should be.

Resolving the Resolution Dilemma

Monitors, computers, and video graphics cards work in tandem. One result of their working relationship is resolution: the number of pixels available per viewable screen. As you likely know, the lowest resolution in common use today on desktop computers is 640 pixels wide by 480 pixels high. Other resolutions include the very common 800×600, the popular 1024×768, and the more luxurious 1280×1024.

If you are designing for wireless devices such as PDAs and smart phones, which have small "baby" faces, you'll need to be even more careful about how you construct your content. Space is so limited in an interface of this nature that breaking up content effectively becomes paramount.

Balance, Harmony, Proportion, and Subtlety

Four critical concepts regarding the placement of objects are the following:

- **Balance.** *Balance is the comparative relationship of one design element with another. Color to space, shape to space, and so on.*

- **Harmony.** *This refers to design elements working together to create visual cohesiveness.*

- **Proportion.** *The comparative relationship of element size.*

- **Subtlety.** *Using moderation in design results in a more reserved effect.*

Assuming a quality video card, driver, and monitor, the higher the numeric value of a resolution is, the crisper and clearer images the monitor will output, although the smaller they will appear. (Of course, this assumes that all the hardware in the setup is functioning properly.) Ideally, web designers have monitors that support a range of resolutions so that they can test the way pages will appear at various resolutions.

Open a web browser. Look at the amount of real estate that it eats up (see Figure 5.1), especially if sidebar panels are activated (see Figure 5.2). The toolbars and status bar of a web browser take up a certain amount of the vertical space. The sidebar and scroll bar consume horizontal space. Yes, end users can customize the toolbars on a browser and gain space, but many web visitors leave their browsers on the default settings that suck up the maximum space allowed.

Figure 5.1 Toolbars and scrollbars take up screen real estate.

For a long time, fixed designs were the rage. To achieve image splicing and similar techniques, tables are fixed at a given pixel width. A significant advantage to this approach is that, with graphically complex sites, images and animations can be cut up into splices to achieve better optimization. The disadvantages to this approach are manifold, however. First, deciding which resolution to design for becomes paramount. This is why you'll come across sites that say, "Best viewed at 800×600" (or some other resolution). This is a terribly ineffective method and should simply not be used.

Figure 5.2 Open up a sidebar panel in your browser, and even more screen real estate is chewed up.

Interestingly, according to modern astronomers, space is finite. This is a very comforting thought—particularly for people who cannot remember where they left things.

—Woody Allen

Another disadvantage is managing space between resolutions. If you optimize a fixed-width design for a low resolution, your design will flush left at higher resolutions (unless you've designated otherwise), leaving a potentially large amount of whitespace to the right (see Figure 5.3). As a result, the space and the content are out of balance.

Some options for dealing with the resolution concerns evolving from fixed-width designs include these:

- Use percentage-based (referred to as *dynamic* or fluid) table layouts.

- Avoid table layouts altogether and use fluid CSS positioning (considered the current ideal practice, if not always possible due to browser version inconsistencies with CSS).

- If you must use fixed-width table designs, consider centering the table (*not* the content, but the actual main layout table itself) on the page, to better balance the remaining space with the page's content.

People also have solved this problem by creating fixed designs for a variety of resolutions and then using a JavaScript sniff-n-route to direct site visitors automatically to the design that will render best in their browsers. This approach has its problems, however: First, it means a heck of a lot more work for you. Second, even at certain resolutions, people resize their browser windows to their comfort levels. Third, some people turn off JavaScript in their browsers.

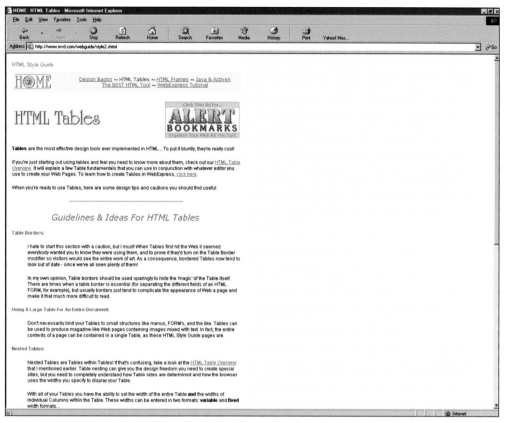

Figure 5.3   Fixed–width design viewed at higher resolution in Internet
             Explorer 6.0. The whitespace on the right is wasted space and is
             terribly unbalanced with the heavy left side of the design.

Getting Rid of the Clutter

I've heard it said that a programmer should never begin to program until he has mapped out a plan. Otherwise, the programming takes a much longer time to execute and debug, especially in complex application development.

To effectively balance content and space, you'll need to map out a plan. This plan should include not only what's going *into* the visual design of your site, but also what's *not* going into it.

I remember a very cool exercise that we did in one of my graduate-level classes. The assignment was to look through magazines and examine ads not for what was in them, but for what was missing. One example was an ad for vitamins geared at a senior audience. What was missing was anything unhealthy or related to age! The models, although mature in age, definitely were fit, trim, and attractive. The scene was a spring-time backyard with a barbecue, a swimming pool, and lots of young people about. This is an example of how what is not added to a design is as—if not more—effective than what is.

Calculated content involves forethought. What's left out of a page results in not only more space, but space that carries significant subliminal impact. Try this: Look at a page you're working on or one that you use regularly. Examine the elements—text, links, graphics, and so forth. What can you take away? Anything that doesn't need to be there *shouldn't* be there. Be ruthless with yourself. If it isn't necessary, leave it out!

> *A human being is a part of the whole, called by us Universe, a part limited in time and space.*
>
> *He experiences himself, his thoughts and feelings as something separated from the rest—a kind of optical delusion of his consciousness. This delusion is a kind of prison, restricting us to our personal desires and to affection for a few persons nearest to us.*
>
> *Our task must be to free from this prison by widening our circle of compassion to embrace all living creatures and the whole nature in its beauty.*
>
> —Albert Einstein

In Figure 5.4, you'll see WebTechniques.com (February 2002). Immediately apparent is that the site is very cramped due to fixed table widths. It's so cramped and cluttered, in fact, that it detracts from the rich information available on the site.

Figure 5.4 A fixed-width design can be too cramped. Look at all the extra whitespace that's wasted as a result. At least the designers did center the table, which makes the space flow around the fixed design in a more balanced fashion.

On the other hand, the internal pages are designed in a more dynamic fashion, making the articles and content much more easily accessible (see Figure 5.5).

Of course, figuring out ways to effectively manage advertising and corporate must-haves is always a bit of a nightmare. But even if you're in such a position, try to be ruthless. Leave the unnecessary out, free up that space, and learn to balance it with other page components (see the sidebar "Proximity, Weight, and Size").

Here's a task for you: Open your favorite image editor and make a canvas that emulates a standard web screen. Create shapes that mimic page elements—logo, header image, navigation, and text. Or, if you prefer, download the practice images provided on the book's web page at **www.molly.com**. Move shapes around the page until you find something that feels balanced and harmonious.

Figure 5.5 Opening up the space makes Lincoln Stein's article much more readable.

Childhood Bedroom

Imagine yourself sitting up in bed, but in the bedroom that you had as a kid. Describe or sketch this childhood room. What are you facing? What's to your left or right? How many windows are in the room? What are the major light sources? Lamps? An overhead light? Is the door open, and is light from the hallway coming in?

What was your favorite thing about your childhood bedroom? Did you feel that you had enough… space? Was that space well used? If you could re-organize your childhood room now, what would you change?

Negative Space

In graphic design, the field behind design elements is described as *negative space* or *whitespace*. The goal is to use this space wisely, controlling how much or how little of it the site visitor gets to see.

You can manage whitespace on a page in numerous technical ways:

- Use cell padding or spacing in table-based layouts.
- Add margins or padding via CSS (a recommended practice).
- Float images within text.
- Use horizontal and vertical spacing with hspace and vspace attributes.
- Mat images on a solid color for additional space.

Proximity, Weight, and Size

Proximity is how close or how far visual pieces are from one another. By controlling the proximity of components on the horizontal and vertical lines of a page, you can emphasize a specific page component, point the eye toward another page component, and create a general balance that's visually satisfying to the visitor.

A component's weight will draw the eye. Images that are too large in relation to other elements on the page create a visual sluggishness, much like that heavy furniture in the small Brooklyn rooms of my young life. You should avoid this kind of graphic problem and go for smaller, crisper images that are more effectively related to other onscreen components.

And despite what anyone tells you, take it from me—size does matter. How big an image should be and how far a page should scroll are critical ideas. Images should never be bigger than a single screen—and, in most cases, they need to be much smaller. There are exceptions to this, but a web author must know what he is doing to get away with designing a large image or a set of images in the context of small screen space.

> *Although presentational elements and attributes such as font, align, border, width, and so on, are allowed in HTML 4.0, 4.01, and XHTML 1.0 Transitional Document types, they are frowned upon in contemporary perspectives on web design. Ideally, you'll be able to choose CSS for presenting your page components and rely on CSS properties for creating additional space on your pages.*

So at what point do you know whether you've got enough space? Pull up a page and ask the following questions:

- Does the page appear balanced?

- Do page components work in harmony? In other words, a header graphic should capture the eye, but the visual space should then lead the eye to the next item of import.

- Is there anything on this page that is unnecessary (still!)?

Certainly, learning to work with space takes some practice—and the more you practice, the more you'll develop a confident eye. I encourage all readers who come to the web as more technical or practical thinkers than creative thinkers to look through various graphic design, art, and architecture books in bookstores and libraries and to see the ways designers have used space, both historically and in contemporary design. Just find your favorite local book repository and spend a few hours there. You'll enjoy the educational benefits and also the sheer joy of hanging out with beautiful and compelling art, architecture, design, and literature.

> *Throw your dreams into space like a kite, and you do not know what it will bring back, a new life, a new friend, a new love, a new country.*
>
> —Anaïs Nin, *The Diaries of Anaïs Nin*

I used to be notoriously upset by rectangles. It's not that I don't use them in design—I do. It's not that I don't value their significance (see Chapter 6, "Embracing Shape"). It's not that they are bad in any way, per se, and in fact can be extremely useful for organizing information.

The concern I have, if not with rectangles themselves, then with the overuse of them in web design, is that every time you use one, you're putting another rectangle inside a rectangle. So, use caution when using rectangles!

I've described the visual web as being a "contained" space. By this, I mean that all the information you see on a web site is inside a rectangle. In fact, more than one rectangle holds a site's information. You not only have the confines of the physical monitor to deal with, but you also have the browser window surrounding your design, as discussed earlier. In a way, surrounding your page with UI elements has a result similar to what happens when you frame visual art.

In fact, the human practice of framing and matting visual objects has a long history. Traditionally, we mat and frame works of art, even a great print or poster that we just happen to like. Sometimes works of art actually are enhanced by their frames.

> *Any great work of art revives and readapts time and space, and the measure of its success is the extent to which it makes you an inhabitant of that world—the extent to which it invites you in and lets you breathe its strange, special air.*
>
> —Leonard Bernstein

Contained Space

My living room has a cathedral ceiling that reaches about two stories high. In that room I have original works of art, all of them matted and framed. The frames enhance the art, and they also provide a focal point for any guest's eye to follow.

Frames are akin to the parameters of a computer monitor; the matting around a picture can be compared to the web browser's toolbars, status bar, and sidebars. But here's the difference: The individual paintings and monoprints hanging in my living room have *plenty* of space between each other. What's more, that space can be measured in feet—even yards.

But consider the contained environment of the computer screen. We're talking about something that you can put your arms around! This is not a place in your home that reaches 8 or more feet high. We're talking inches here. So, the more rectangles there are in the space, and the more stuff there is in the space, the less space there is.

Less space means more clutter and clutter upsets a lot of people. Personally, if I'm uncomfortable with or upset about a site's design, I'm very rarely going to wade through it unless *absolutely* necessary. I'm simply outta there.

Favorite Space

Describe your ideal environment. Cityscape? Farmland? Woodsy back road? Write one paragraph or find a photograph that conveys your ideal sense of space. Put this near your work area as a source of inspiration when developing your sites.

Some simple but important tricks for avoiding the overcontainment of web space include these:

- Use borders within table layouts sparingly. Borders can sometimes enhance tabular data, and it can also draw the eye to important sidebar information, but generally speaking, you'll want to avoid overuse of borders in layout design.

- Avoid bordered frames.

- Use borders around images only where appropriate in a design. A better choice is to find an interesting (but subtle) photographic edge effect.

Favorite Season

Space is as much a sensation as it is a physical reality. Think about how the seasons make you feel. If you're somewhere cold and gray in winter, there's a sense of enclosure. But a gorgeous spring day feels wide open. What's your favorite season? Why? Draw images or go through some magazines and find images of this time of year. Then, create a design that captures your favorite season and the way it makes you feel.

Check your most recent work: Is there enough space? Have you accommodated a variety of screen resolutions? Have you balanced text and objects so that the eye is led where you want it to go? Does everything on your page have a good raison d'étre?

If so, you've improved your use of space. On today's cluttered, busy web, your site visitors will appreciate a great, spacious place to hang out for a while.

Integrated Design

Once you've gone through the exercises in this chapter and gained insight into how to better approach space from a conceptual standpoint, consider that color and space combine to create visual interest on a page. Imagine white text on a red background or a black hourglass against a white background. There exists an integrated relationship here, as the field's space is modified by the text or figure, and the text or figure is influenced by the colors used. By effectively combining color and space, you can bring elements into prominence or make them subtler within the design.

Now that I've impressed upon you the importance of space, balance, and harmony, I have one more piece of advice. Once you feel confident that you've gained the skills to properly use space in a design, it's time to attempt designs that defy traditional approaches. Purposely break the guidelines, but only once you feel truly confident that you understand them.

CHAPTER 6

Embracing Shape

Humans have long been fascinated with shape. We seek to examine shape mathematically and aesthetically. Our fascination with the abundance of shape in nature means that shape has been studied and recorded for centuries. Shape is reflected in science and the humanities: math, mechanics (see Figure 6.1), physics, art, and architecture (see Figure 6.2). Music has even been said to contain shape.

As with the use of color and space, shape in design can work to elicit strong responses from the audience. Knowing what thoughts shapes can evoke can empower you to use shape within your work to help influence and guide your site visitors.

Using shape effectively in a design can result in a wide range of psychological reactions that can motivate, inspire, and provide an enjoyable adventure, even if the audience is unaware of why those specific feelings and subsequent actions arise.

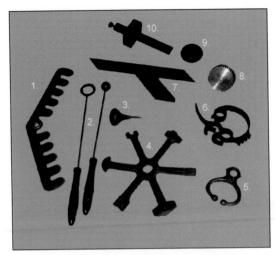

Figure 6.1   Shapes in the history of mechanical tools. Can you guess what these things are?
(See the end of the chapter for answers.)

Figure 6.2   Shapes in a Tunisian floor mosaic, Third Century A.D.

> *The artist is a receptacle for the emotions that come from all over the place: from the sky, from the Earth, from a scrap of paper, from a passing shape, from a spider's web.*
>
> —Pablo Picasso

Shapes are subtler in their influence than some aspects of design, such as color, but are similarly subject to the issues of culture, economic climate, and individual perception. By themselves, shapes are just shapes, but throughout human history we have used them—whether by accident or on purpose—in art, architecture, and of course visual design. Just as our emotional perception of color will be determined by many influences, so it is with shape. And, as with color, a symbolism of shapes has emerged describing predominant archetypal meanings. Designers tap into these archetypes in order to convey specific expression within their designs.

Table 6.1 describes common shapes and what archetypal influences can generally be expected from them.

Table 6.1 Shape Meanings at a Glance

Shape	General Symbolism
Circle	Connection, community, wholeness, endurance, movement, safety. Often refers to the feminine: warmth, comfort, sensuality, and love.
Rectangle	Order, logic, containment, security. Suggest mass, volume, and solids.
Triangle	Energy, power, balance, law, science, religion. Often refers to the masculine: strength, aggression, and dynamic movement.

Shape and Cultural Paradox

While the predominant archetypes described in the table are very strong and can be readily used to some predictable end in design, it's important to be aware of symbolic paradox, which arises from difference in culture and perspective. This is especially true when we look at religious symbols such as the cross and the Star of David, which can evoke comfort, faith, and pride in those who embrace those symbols within their lives; or conversely represent an enemy, a war, or some entity to be feared.

Before the terrorist attacks on the U.S. on September 11, 2001, the two rectangular towers of the World Trade Center represented a symbol of pride and human triumph—they were, after all, the tallest buildings in the world at the time they were built. After their destruction, the images of two towering rectangles leave an entirely different mark on the eyes of the world. For many of us, it is a symbol of tragedy, for some, those rectangular images are now a symbol of triumph against tyranny.

Collages

Working under the theory that technical people tend to be linear thinkers and visual people tend to think in more of an iterative way, collages can be a good way for both sides to gain a better understanding of shape.

Pretend for a moment that you are not a designer or programmer or whatever you do, and that you live a completely different life. Think big. Then go through magazines or surf the web for images that fill this imaginary life with pictures of palm trees, surfboards, big trophies, sailboats, or whatever you fantasize about.

Lay out the story of your imaginary life in collage form. As you go through the exercise, notice the shapes that combine to create those trees, surfboards, and trophies. Do you see a pattern? Does a particular shape show up consistently within your creations? If you see a specific shape show up numerous times, what do you think that means? For example, if you tend to have a lot of rectangles, perhaps it reflects a desire for more grounding, or a reflection that you are in fact a very grounded person.

The Circle

A circle is a closed curve consisting of all points at a given distance from some fixed point, which is considered the circle's center.

In helping others, we shall help ourselves, for whatever good we give out completes the circle and comes back to us.

—Flora Edwards

You'll possibly remember these parts of a circle from geometry class:

- **Radius.** Any line connecting the center with any point on the circle's curve.

- **Circumference.** The length of the circle's arc.

- **Chord.** A line segment with ends lying on the circle's circumference.

- **Diameter.** A chord through the center of the circle.

Figure 6.3 shows the anatomy of a basic circle.

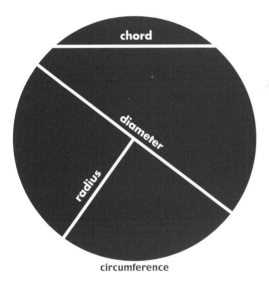

Figure 6.3 The circle, with several parts described.

The circle and its components are abundant in design. From an archetypal perspective, circles convey important meanings:

- Heaven
- Eternity
- Universe
- Connection
- Community
- Wholeness
- Endurance
- Movement
- Safety

Circles have been said to be feminine, and their psychological influence suggests warmth, comfort, sensuality, sexuality, and love.

Consider what type of sites might benefit from a design incorporating a circle. Some ideas I came up with were: a community web site, a spirituality web site, a women's web site, and a dating web site.

Landscape

Shape in landscape is everywhere. Take a walk around your neighborhood. Look at how the buildings, houses, trees, bushes, and even lawns all fit together.

Which shapes stand out to you as interesting, regardless of the size? Even look at the walkways, the entryways to the buildings, and the front steps. All these shapes were purposely chosen by the landscape artists and building architects who designed them.

The Rectangle

A rectangle is a closed figure bounded by four sides and having four right angles. A square is a rectangle with equal sides (see Figure 6.4).

In design, rectangles suggest powerful meanings, possibly because of their rigidity and specificity. Some of these meanings include the ones in this list:

- Order

- Logic

- Containment

- Security

Rectangles also suggest mass, volume, and solids.

rectangle

square

Figure 6.4   A rectangle and a square.

Consider the types
of web sites you could
create using rectangles
as a dominant shape.
Some site types would
be a banking site, a
security services site,
and a site for conserva-
tive organizations.

"Here's to the crazy ones. The misfits. The rebels. The trouble-makers. The round heads in the square holes. The ones who see things differently. They're not fond of rules. And they have no respect for the status quo. You can quote them. Disagree with them. Glorify or vilify them. But the only thing you can't do is ignore them. Because they change things. They push the human race forward. And while some may see them as the crazy ones, we see genius. Because the people who are crazy enough to think they can change the world, are the ones who do. Think Different."

—Apple

Rocks, Shells, or Leaves

Find five small, interesting rocks, shells, or leaves. Lay them on a surface and look at how they are similar and how they are different.

This is nature's way of making shape choices. What made you pick each one? If you used leaves, you can take it a step further by pressing them between wax paper and saving them in a book or putting them up on a wall in your work area. If you chose rocks and shells, you can put them into a glass jar and keep them by your desk for inspiration. Look at the variety of shapes. How can they enhance the design you're working on today?

From a mathematical point of view, the triangle is a figure bound by three line segments. The sides of these segments intersect at three points, known as the *vertices*.

> *The hand, the heart, and the head*
> *form a triangle that can bring untold*
> *happiness, if used together. One alone*
> *is not much service, any more than*
> *one blade of a scissors.*
>
> —William C. Hunter

Any segment in a triangle can be considered the triangle's base. Other triangular features include these:

- **Altitude.** The distance from the triangle's base to the opposite vertex.

- **Median.** The line segment joining the midpoint of a side to the opposite vertex.

Figure 6.5 shows a triangle with its basic components.

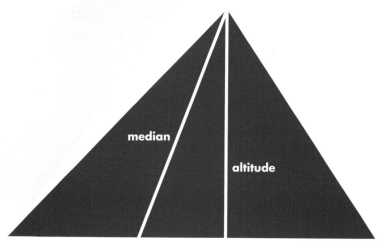

Figure 6.5   A triangle.

Various types of triangles exist:

- **Equilateral.** A triangle in which all three angles are equal.

- **Isosceles.** A triangle with two equal angles.

- **Scalene.** A triangle with three different angles.

- **Right.** A triangle with one right angle.

- **Acute.** A triangle in which all three angles are acute.

- **Obtuse.** A triangle which is neither acute nor contains a right angle.

Figure 6.6 shows each type of triangle.

Triangles can be used to represent a number of ideas, including these:

- Energy

- Power

- Balance

- Law

- Science

- Religion

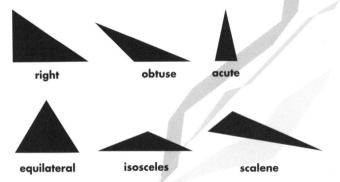

Figure 6.6 Equilateral, isosceles, scalene, right, acute, and obtuse triangles.

Triangles are thought to be masculine, implying qualities such as strength, aggression, and dynamic movement. The direction of a triangle also influences its meaning. Triangles with a predominant angle to one side will encourage the eye to move that direction. Triangles that have their highest angle at the top invoke more uplifting ideas; triangles that appear to slope downward invoke a less positive emotion.

Consider how triangles might enhance a site's visual design. You can use triangles to direct the eye up or down, or side to side. You can integrate triangles into your design any time you want to communicate movement, direction, power, or strength.

Attention Sports Fans

Go to any sports game, or find one on TV. Notice how the team works together as a group. For example, if you like football, watch how the different formations start, shift, and cover the field on each play. In baseball, notice the shapes on the field—referred to as a diamond, of course. Shape is everywhere!

Sorrowful Triangles

In Nazi concentration camps, triangles commonly were used to identify prisoners. Each prisoner in the camp wore a triangle with a specific color that reflected the reason for his incarceration in the camp.

A green triangle represented a regular criminal. Red triangles were worn by political prisoners. The familiar Star of David is made up of two triangles. Jewish prisoners wore yellow Stars of David to identify them. The pink triangle (facing downward) represented homosexual prisoners. The lowest prisoner on the social hierarchy within the camps wore a yellow Star of David under a superimposed pink triangle. This represented a gay Jew.

Source: Rainbow Icon Archive,
www.enqueue.com/ria/triangles.html

Integrated Design: Combined and Partial Shapes

Shapes can also be combined for greater impact. Think about using a circle and a triangle in combination—the results can convey an energetic, dynamic community. Or, combine a circle and a rectangle to express warmth and security.

The impact of shape and shape combinations has been demonstrated in a wide range of applications. The design of automobiles, buildings, product packaging, and company logos all include shape as enticement. In the late 1980s and early 1990s, car manufacturers became aware of the fact that many more women were making decisions about auto purchases. As a result, car designs began to include more curves (see Figure 6.7).

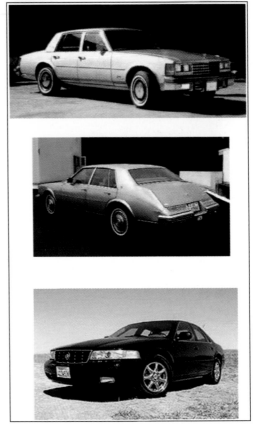

Figure 6.7   Shape in car design over time: square, angled, and curved versions of the Cadillac Seville, 1976, 1981, and 1998.

> *Imagination is more important than knowledge. Knowledge is limited. Imagination encircles the world.*
>
> —Albert Einstein

The impact of shape is perhaps most obvious when dealing with logo design. One of my favorite examples of the impact of subtle shape combination is FedEx's logo (see Figure 6.8). Look at the shape formed by the space between the *E* and the *x*. It's an arrow pointing to the right. Unless you've had this pointed out to you by someone, it's highly unlikely that you've ever noticed it—but, rest assured, this is no accident! Think now about which shapes have combined to make up this arrow. It's a rectangle and a triangle, meaning "secure movement."

Color, of course, is combined with shape for impact. FedEx's express overnight logo is colored a purple-blue with orange—blue for security and orange for action. When FedEx recently added ground service, the resulting logo colors were blue and green, with the green representing the ground.

The use of partial shape is very important, too. Instead of using whole shapes, partial shapes such as arcs or the angles of a triangle or rectangle can be used in design to invoke certain ideas. The curves of Girlshop's design are direct representations of the female curves, and the general archetypal symbolism of the circle (see Figure 6.9). If you compare this to the more angular design of Guyshop (Figure 6.10), you can easily see the use of partial shapes in action.

See the arrow?!?

Figure 6.8 Shape combining in the FedEx logo.

Figure Quiz Key

Did you manage to guess what the mechanical objects in Figure 6.1 are? Here are the answers:

1. Guard for polishing brass buttons, made of brass.

2. Thermal expansion demonstrator. Brass with painted wood handles. The ball fits through the ring when cold, but not when hot.

3. Engraving tool, steel with wood handle.

4. Oil delivery tool of nonsparking bronze.

5. Nose ring for a cow or bull, made of brass. The loop is for a rope; you can push the button to open the ring portion wider.

6. Cast-iron brass knuckles. These are in an unusual form, possibly to avoid illegality.

7. Carpenter's 45° square of steel and mahogany.

8. Machinist's dividers, made of steel.

9. Cast-iron paperweight for a news stand in the shape and style of a Smith Brothers licorice cough drop (remember those?).

10. Carpenter's scribe made of brass and rosewood.

Typically, a partial shape retains the archetypal meanings of its parent shape, but this depends upon how the shape is used. An arc can imply the warmth and involvement found in a community, or it can imply a broken community; it depends upon how you as the designer choose to use it, how you color it, and where you put it within the space of the design.

Shape combining and the use of partial shape is where designing with shape really begins. So, it's important to learn to combine the technical components of shape for maximum impact.

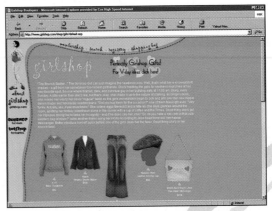

Figure 6.9   Curves at GirlShop.Com show how partial shapes typically imply the same meanings as whole shapes.

Figure 6.10   The more angular Guyshop.com.

CHAPTER 7

Using Typography

As you read these very words, you are responding to the power of type. Since primitive times, humans have left indelible marks on the earth. From the earliest pictographs in cave dwellings to the modern use of type as an art form, the study of typography has been an integrated study because it reflects so many aspects of human nature and expression.

Type is the following:

- **Mechanical.** Traditional typesetting is a mechanized process.

- **Mathematical.** Letterforms, the space between lines of type, and the space between letters are each determined using mathematics.

- **Communicative.** Letters come together to communicate via written language.

- **Emotional.** The human psyche responds to what it reads. We can laugh, cry, become angry, or be uplifted by what is communicated to us via type.

- **Artistic.** Type can be used as design and not language. While words carry meaning, letters and words are also curves, angles, space, shape, and color.

Our interpretation of life results in complicated and variegated expressions. What is represented symbolically is filled with the emotion of its creators, and the symbol in turn evokes emotion from those that are exposed, react, and respond to it.

Human language begins, and still remains, with pictographs and letter-forms. These things serve as a representation of our histories and cultures via language. Type fascinates and absorbs. Somehow, the intimacy that emerges from human relation to language inspires enormous commitment. Type is loved, studied, and even argued over.

Type is an extension of this relationship with language—intimate, evolutionary. Typography itself is complicated, emotional, and variegated.

> *Letter shapes and letter sizes are reasonably limited. But beyond that we rely primarily on emotion.*
>
> —Gerard Unger, from *Legible?*

A Brief History of Digital Type

To better understand the aesthetic and technical aspects of typography, look to the history of type. It is not surprising that what we know as digital fonts today got their inspiration from handwritten, calligraphic fonts of many years ago.

Historians point to four passages in history that have been profoundly important to growth spurts in type and type technology. The first was in the fifteenth century, when the job of creating written documents moved literally from the hands of scribes into Gutenberg's printing press. Many describe this not only as an important passage in the history of type, but as a passage for humanity itself as we began the process of mass printing and archiving of human expression.

> *…one thing absolutely necessary for working with fonts is knowing their history—what came after what and, more importantly, why.*
>
> —Dmitry Kirsanov, *The World of Fonts*

The industrial revolution saw new types of mechanics applied to older ideas. During this period, Gutenberg's printing system—which actually remained relatively untouched for several hundred years—became mechanized. Other aspects of typesetting, such as the point system of measurement, emerged at this time.

The third important passage in typographic history came about with the use of photography in graphic design. The ability to project characters onto photographic paper enabled typesetters in the mid-twentieth century to do new things with type, such as transparencies and characters that overlapped. This period is important because it marks the transition from organic type to typography as most of us work with it today.

Enter the digital age. As computer technology improves, so does our ability to create type via digital means. We began with bitmapped fonts, which use specific pixels to produce letterforms. Now, vector graphics enable us to work with scalable fonts. Scalable fonts give us a great deal of flexibility in how we size and process fonts. Additional technologies, such as TrueType, give greater control of even the smallest representational portions of a character, resulting in improved clarity of a typeface as it appears on screen.

The information in this chapter focuses on Latin-based character sets. Many other international character sets and fonts exist as well.

Around the House

Typography is practically ubiquitous. It appears in so many aspects of our lives that we might not notice it. Wherever you're sitting reading this book, look around and see where type is used. I'm in my office. I see a wall calendar, which uses a variety of type styles. There are shipping boxes with various printed information. My beer label has multiple typefaces on it, as does my tea mug, left over from breakfast. Look at type around the house, and then in the world. You might be surprised at how often you are looking at varieties of type and type styles without realizing it!

Primary Principles in Typography

Despite its long history, typography may be an elusive portion of the web professional's daily work. Part of this results from technological limitations and part results from not being exposed to the history and practice of typography.

Families and Faces

Classifying type is a complex concern and has taken a variety of forms. There are so many different kinds of type that grouping them into sensible containers so as to learn and identify them is very helpful.

Although my classification will likely differ from others you'll find, I like to organize type when discussed in the context of web typography as follows:

- **Category.** A type category is the master group or family. (See Figure 7.1.) Think of this as a typeface's ethnic heritage. The master family from which a typeface descends influences its physical attributes—its shape, line, and form. Examples of categories would be serif, sans serif, and fantasy.

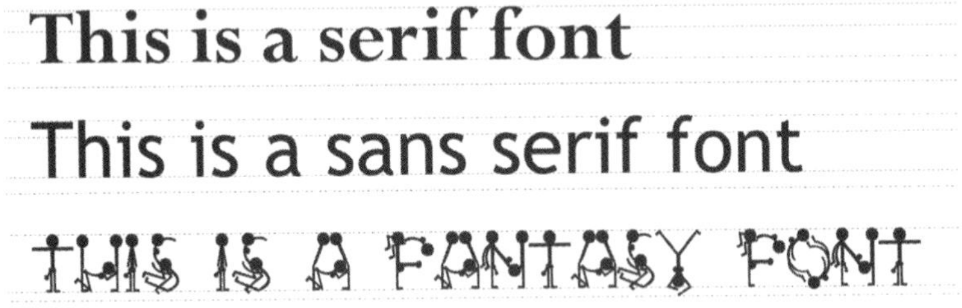

This is a serif font

This is a sans serif font

THIS IS A FANTASY FONT

Figure 7.1 Type category examples.

- **Family.** Within a master category are the names of the individual families. Families contain similarities in their individual type forms. For example, all of the members of a family will have similar curves and lines, (See Figure 7.2.) Examples of families include Arial, Times, and Garamond.

- **Face.** A face is the unique style within a family, such as Arial Bold, Arial Bold Italic or Times New Roman Bold, Times New Roman Italic. (See Figure 7.3.)

This is Times New Roman
This is Arial

Figure 7.2 Type family examples.

Times New Roman Italic
Arial Bold

Figure 7.3 Type face examples.

As shown in Figure 7.4, type categories include the following:

- **Serif.** This is a familiar standard group identified by smaller strokes or flourishes used to embellish individual letters. Historically, serif faces emerged from handwritten documents of old.

- **Sans Serif.** A group common to web design is the sans serif category. "Sans" means "without" in Latin, so these families tend to be rounded and have no flourishes.

- **Monospaced.** Each letter in a face occupies the same amount of space as every other. This is often called a typewriter font, because it resembles the evenly spaced type of those old-fashioned contraptions.

- **Script.** This category includes all families that resemble handwriting.

> *Scripts are emotional, lyrical, even passionate communicators. Words that are set in script faces make an impact far greater than their literal meaning could convey.*
>
> —Scripts: A Type of Passion, *Fonts.com*

- **Decorative.** Sometimes referred to as fantasy, this group has special decorative features such as dots, strokes, and other designs that are applied to the families and faces.

- **Symbolic.** Also referred to as dingbats, this category contains fonts that are either pictographic or that have special character sets.

Many designers spend their entire lives learning how to design with and create type, illustrating type's power as a design element. Choose the right type, and your work will have the impact you're after. Choose a clashing or inappropriate typeface, and your work will be unattractive, ineffective, or worse, boring.

This is a serif font

This is a sans serif font

`This is a monospaced font`

This is a script font

THIS IS A FANTASY FONT

Figure 7.4 Type categories in detail.

Type Anatomy

Type anatomy is the science of letterforms. This science looks at the measurement of characters from their foundation (*baseline*) to their top portion. Type anatomy also examines the various kinds of strokes, flourishes, and spaces in characters. (See Figure 7.5.)

The elements of type anatomy are

- **Arm.** A horizontal or diagonal stroke on the upper part of a character.

- **Apex.** Where two strokes join in a pointed fashion, as with A.

- **Ascender.** Any part of a lowercase letter that goes beyond the allowed lowercase height for that font.

- **Bar.** Horizontal strokes across a letter, such as in H or A.

- **Beak.** The beak-shaped stroke on L, T, and E. It is much like a *spur*.

- **Bowl.** Curved strokes that cause enclosed space. This enclosed space is, as you'll soon read, referred to as a *counter*.

- **Cap Height.** The height of a capital letter from its baseline to the top of its cap.

- **Counter.** The enclosed or partially enclosed space caused by letters with curved strokes.

- **Descender.** Any part of a character that falls below the baseline.

- **Ear.** A small stroke appearing on a lowercase g at the top right of the letter.

- **Finial.** The end tip of a loop, found on C and e.

- **Leg.** A horizontal or diagonal stroke on the lower part of a character.

- **Link.** The stroke that connects the top and bottom of a lowercase g.

- **Loop.** The looping, bottom portion of a lowercase g.

- **Serif.** Strokes that adorn serif typefaces.

- **Shoulder.** The curving stroke that creates the rounded portion of h, m, and n.

- **Spine.** The center stroke of an S.

- **Spur.** The small stroke hanging off of a capital G.

- **Stem.** A vertical or diagonal stroke in a character.

- **Stress.** The way a curve thickens.

- **Stroke.** A line on a typeface. Strokes can be straight or curved.

- **Swash.** Any kind of expressive flourish.

- **Tail.** The portion of a Q that falls below the baseline, and the diagonal portion of a capital R.

- **Terminal.** Any end of a stroke without a serif.

- **X-height.** The height of lowercase letters.

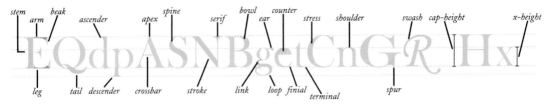

stem   beak   ascender   apex   spine   serif   bowl   ear   counter   stress   shoulder   swash   cap-height   x-height

arm

leg   tail   descender   crossbar   stroke   link   loop   finial   terminal   spur

Figure 7.5 Anatomy of type.

Leading

Typography also concerns itself with the space between lines, which is called *leading* (pronounced led-ing) or *line-height*. (See Figure 7.6.) Specifically, leading is measured from the baseline of a line to the top of the x-height of the line below it. How close or how far one line is from another tremendously influences readability and emotional response to the visual communication.

As a general rule, leading set close to the type's own point size is suitable for body text. If leading is set at too great a distance, readability can be compromised. Using unusual leading for impact is effective in short sections of text, such as headers or sidebars, or if you're using type as a portion of design, rather than specifically as text necessary to be read and understood.

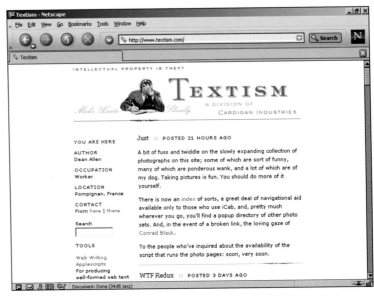

Figure 7.6 Dean Allen's Textism uses Cascading Style Sheets to gain a slightly wider line-height than the default. The result is an elegant design that is also easy to read.

Kerning and Letterspacing

Kerning is the space between individual letters within a font. In default settings for some typefaces, you'll notice that letters touch one another, and this can sometimes interfere with readability. Although the problem can affect any font, it occurs frequently with serif fonts.

Kerning allows a typesetter to adjust this space. (See Figure 7.7.) Adjustments require accessing information contained within the font in a *kerning table*. Kerning tables contain mathematical information related to the units of each letterform within the font.

Figure 7.7   Kerning type in Adobe Illustrator. The top example is auto-kerned. In the bottom example, I used the Character palette to modify the kerning between the letters.

Letterspacing is the horizontal space between letters. In other words, you don't have to access the kerning table to set a letter farther from or closer to another over the entire word. This is also referred to as *tracking*. It's a less specific way to manage spacing, and differs from kerning in that you can't control individual letters within a word.

As with leading, letterspacing influences the readability of a passage. (See Figure 7.8.) While the use of spacing can add visual interest to a page, unusual space values should be restricted to decorative or short bursts of text. Body text requires normal spacing to be attractive and comfortable to the reader.

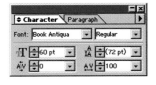

Figure 7.8   Spacing type in Adobe Illustrator. The top example is normal spacing; the bottom example shows how I've used the Character palette to alter the spacing of the entire word.

Type Form

Typefaces have specific attributes. These attributes are referred to as *form*. Form specifically relates to the shape and direction in which a given typeface is presented and includes weight, width, and posture.

- **Weight.** Numerous weight classes exist in type, including the general classes with which you may already be familiar: *regular*, *bold*, and *light*. Regular is the average weight class, simple and unadorned. Bold is heavier and slightly wider than regular type-face and is used to emphasize text. Light typeface is slender and, as its name implies, lighter than regular typeface. It also has a subtler impact than regular or bold forms and can help achieve a very clean look.

- **Width.** Typefaces can have a variety of widths. The two most common type widths are *condensed* and *expanded*. A condensed, or compressed, form has a tighter letterform width than the standard version, and an expanded, or extended, typeface is wider than the standard version.

- **Posture.** Type posture refers specifically to the angle at which the type is set. *Italic* type, as you know, slants to the right and, like bold, emphasizes text. *Oblique* is the digital manipulation of a normal face into a facsimile of italicization, which is designed as a specific part of that typeface. Posture conveys a great deal, making a word, phrase or heading seem active or static, serious or whimsical.

Very often, how light or heavy, wide or narrow, stooped or straight we are depends largely upon our heritage, or, the way we position ourselves. This is true of type, as well.

Size, Proportion, and Direction

Another consideration when working with typefaces is their size and proportion to one another—and to other elements on a page.

Type is measured in a variety of ways, including *points* or *pixels*. Point measurement is based on print measurement, whereas pixel measurement uses a computer's pixel-based technology to interpret point size. What's more, ems and percentages, available in Cascading Style Sheets (CSS), offer type that is scalable by resolution. (For more information on CSS, see Chapter 9, "The Technology of Design: Cascading Style Sheets.")

The size and proportion of a typeface is important to style and design. Size can help indicate what role the typeface is playing on the page: Larger type is used for headers, medium sizes for body text, small sizes for notes and less emphasized information, such as copyright notices.

Varying type size on a page is important, but just as important is keeping that variation consistent. You're looking for the visual interest and practical results that having different sizes of fonts on a page provide. You don't want to overwhelm your visitor with too much contrast or complete chaos.

Type direction refers to the direction in which a typeface is set. You can set typefaces to run horizontally left to right, vertically up and down with, you can create type that runs along a curved path, and you can set type to be free-form.

Special Issues in Typography

With an idea of the fundamental concerns in typography, we can more readily move into the electronic world and discuss how type works on screen, and of course, on the web. Detailed information about the technical and decorative use of type can be very helpful for the web professional attempting to understand in greater detail how to use type to effectively design and communicate.

Anti-Aliasing and Font Smoothing

Although vector fonts are scalable, most fonts that are used in static web graphics are exported as bitmaps, which means that they are made up of individual pixels of information. As a result of bitmapping, screen fonts can often appear jagged. (See Figure 7.9.)

To address this issue, designers use a technique known as *anti-aliasing*. This technique is the smoothing of those jagged edges by blurring and lightening certain pixels to make the results appear even. Anti-aliasing features are available in most imaging programs for print and web.

Figure 7.9   To show the individual pixels, and the potential jagged results, I magnified a letterform.

Combining Type and Typographic Features

Type can be combined in a variety of ways for effect. In fact, gifted type designers understand this approach and use it to create beautiful, effective designs. You can combine many aspects of type, including faces, type weights, and sizes.

The emotional impact of combining type is interesting, because you can create harmonious relationships, discordant ones, and contrasting ones.

Harmonious relationships are built on similarities. When combining type, a good way to achieve harmony is to stick within a family, yet use a variety of weights and posturing for effect. As you become more adept at working with type, you can be more experimental with the faces, but using weights and posture for effect still remains interesting (See Figure 7.10).

Figure 7.10   The Buffalo Exchange web site uses color, capitalization, and weight to achieve typographic interest (**www.buffaloexchange.com**).

Discordant relationships are built on conflict. In type, this discord results when fonts that are too similar are mixed together. This creates a potentially disturbing and problematic design.

But, contrasting relationships are often the most interesting, because you can choose typefaces that are radically different from one another and ultimately have a full range of expressive options as a result. (See Figure 7.11.) If you're not a skilled graphic designer with a typographic background, however, you'll need practice at type combining, and a lot of exposure to various effective examples of typographic design. Otherwise, you run the risk of creating a design that is confusing or inappropriate for the content.

Generally speaking, avoid mixing fonts from the same category. Don't mix Garamond and Times, for example, because they are both serif fonts. Fonts from the same category are often too similar to create contrast, which you want, and too dissimilar to allow for continuity and legibility, which is usually necessary.

One way of combining type on a page without running into problems is to choose one sans serif and one serif face. Use the sans serif for headers, and the serif face for the body text. You can also switch this around and see if the results are acceptable. This method has been in use in print for a very long time, and creates a clear contrast between what is a header, and what is body text.

Figure 7.11 Type contrast at Juxtinteractive.com (**www.juxtinteractive.com**).

Readability and Legibility

There's a lot of conversation in the web world about read-ability. For web designers, this simply refers to the site visitor's ease of use when encountering the text portions of a document.

In typography, readability and legibility have subtly different meanings. In an article for Fonts.com, Allan Haley writes how readability and legibility are two very different things. He describes readability as being more dependent upon the *use* of a typeface rather than the design of the typeface itself. On the other hand, legibility is the ability to distinguish one letter from another within a given typeface.

As Haley goes on to point out, typefaces are not always designed to be legible. Type is often designed to be artistic, unusual, or whimsical in order to appeal to the varied tastes of typographers creating type that isn't concerned with readability. In those cases, the type becomes the design, and the emphasis is much less on what the type is trying to say than the way it looks.

> *We shouldn't confuse legibility with communication.*
>
> —David Carson, *The End of Print*

Emphasis and Justification

To emphasize type is to make a set of characters more apparent in some way than those around it. This is helpful in digital communication when a word or phrase requires some emphasis.

Two primary ways of using emphasis in type design are to

- Change the posture of the type by making it italic or oblique

- Change the weight of the type, especially by making it heavier

A special concern with emphasis while setting graphic type is that you use the font's actual italic, oblique, or bold faces. Do not rely on the computer program's style options. These digitally alter the normal weight of the face, rather than access the bold form of the face.

Justification plays yet another part in the way your use of type influences communication. (See Figure 7.12.) The four main types of justification are

- **Left.** Also referred to as *ragged right*, this is the most familiar justification in use.

- **Right.** All lines of text are flushed to the right of the page, leaving a ragged left margin.

- **Center.** All lines of text are centered between the margins. The centering of text is very useful for short bursts of information, such as headlines, callouts, and captions.

- **Justified.** Type is flush to both the right and left margins. This is achieved by using additional spaces between words within a paragraph. Justification is good for columnar layouts, where the width of the column is not so long so as to introduce additional, confusing space.

It must have been a little after three o'clock in the afternoon that it happened--the afternoon of June 3rd, 1916. It seems incredible that all that I have passed through--all those weird and terrifying experiences--should have been encompassed within so short a span as three brief months. Rather might I have experienced a cosmic cycle, with all its changes and evolutions for that which I have seen with my own eyes in this brief interval of time--things that no other mortal eye had seen before, glimpses of a world past, a world dead, a world so long dead that even in the lowest Cambrian stratum no trace of it remains. Fused with the melting inner crust, it has passed forever beyond the ken of man other than in that lost pocket of the earth whither fate has borne me and where my doom is sealed. I am here and here must remain.

After reading this far, my interest, which already had been stimulated by the finding of the manuscript, was approaching the boiling-point. I had come to Greenland for the summer, on the advice of my physician, and was slowly being bored to extinction, as I had thoughtlessly neglected to bring sufficient reading-matter. Being an indifferent fisherman, my enthusiasm for this form of sport soon waned; yet in the absence of other forms of recreation I was now risking my life in an entirely inadequate boat off Cape Farewell at the southernmost extremity of Greenland.

Greenland! As a descriptive appellation, it is a sorry joke--but my story has nothing to do with Greenland, nothing to do with me; so I shall get through with the one and the other as rapidly as possible.

The inadequate boat finally arrived at a precarious landing, the natives, waist-deep in the surf, assisting. I was carried ashore, and while the evening meal was being prepared, I wandered to and fro along the rocky, shattered shore. Bits of surf-harried beach clove the worn granite, or whatever the rocks of Cape Farewell may be composed of, and as I followed the ebbing tide down one of these soft stretches, I saw the thing. Were one to bump into a Bengal tiger in the ravine behind the Bimini Baths, one could be no more surprised than was I to see a perfectly good quart thermos bottle turning and twisting in the surf of Cape Farewell at the southern extremity of Greenland. I rescued it, but I was soaked above the knees doing it; and then I sat down in the sand and opened it, and in the long twilight read the manuscript, neatly written and tightly folded, which was its contents.

Figure 7.12   The four styles of type justification: Left (shown at top), Right, Center, and Justified (shown at bottom).

No one has figured out quite how to use type well on the web. Part of this is born from technological limitations, and some of the problem is the result of many people with no exposure to typographic principles doing web work.

Fortunately, with better support for presentational technologies such as CSS, there's a lot more we can control about our typographic designs. While fonts still need to be resident on an individual's machine to effectively display, the quality of control that CSS offers over sizing, leading, spacing, width, posture, and other typographic features is a huge step in the right direction for individuals interested in creating great typographic designs for the web.

One ongoing design debate is whether serif or sans serif fonts are more readable. General consensus for print is that common serif fonts, such as Times New Roman, are excellent for body text. It is possible that the serif strokes create a line for the eye to follow, thereby acting as a visual guide. No one really knows why readability tests have shown serif fonts to be superior for body text in print. Many print designers have, as a result, been taught that they should usually use serif fonts for body and sans serif, with their rounded, strong letterforms, for headers.

Of course, print and screen are very different. Anecdotal evidence is piling up that shows most people find sans serif fonts easier to read onscreen, especially common sans serif fonts such as Arial, Helvetica, and Verdana. Verdana's wide letterforms and broad support have made it especially popular in recent years.

Type and the Web

Newsstand

Take a trip to your local newsstand, bookstore, or magazine shop. While scanning the magazine rack, notice the different fonts and layouts used on the different publications. How do women's magazines compare to, say, auto magazines or home and garden magazines? Try looking at the type treatments of technical journals as compared to news magazines. Find a very technical treatment and visually compare it with a more creative one. Which appeals to you, and why?

Integrated Design

So, how does type integrate with other design elements discussed? The use of color with type, the relationship of type and space, and the shapes that type can create are powerful examples of how typography is most effective and innovative when used in an integrated fashion with other design elements. Take a closer look:

- **Font Color.** Color is important in type design because the use of different colors will influence the way a word is perceived in relation to another. Warm colors, such as reds and oranges, come forward and command our attention. Cool colors, such as blue, tend to be effective but not overt.

  According to most designers, contrasting warm and cool colors can bring attention to certain words, while detracting emphasis from others.

A welcoming block of text is one of even colour—that is to say, consistent in overall tone: dense settings give off darker colour, loose settings are light. The ideal colour is defined by personal taste, but evenness and consistency go straight to the goal of unhindered reading.

—Dean Allen, The Destination Matters More than the Journey

- **Fonts and Space.** The way you use fonts will affect the white space on a page. This is especially true when you alter the sizing and proportion of a font, or when you modify justification.

- **Fonts and Shape.** One of the most delightful things about fonts is that they naturally produce interesting shapes. Combine that with color and a sense of space, and you can come up with compelling, unusual designs that break away from the mundane.

Figures 7.13 through 7.15 show how all these concepts work together on the **www.jiong.com** site.

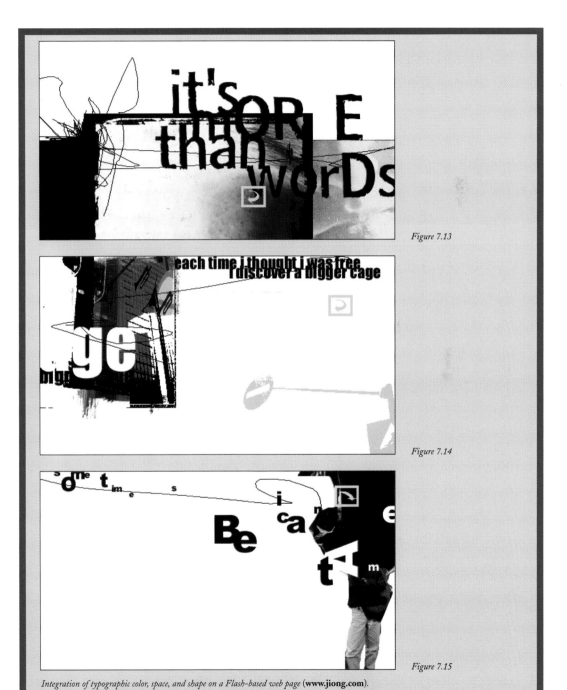

Figure 7.13

Figure 7.14

Figure 7.15

Integration of typographic color, space, and shape on a Flash-based web page (**www.jiong.com**).

PART III

Integration Primer for the Artistically Inclined

p

...then who marks up
...arkup languages, it's rare to
...s with documents only. Instead,
...HTML or working with visual editors,
...Adobe GoLive. Developers might also
...rkup, even though their primary focus is
...opment.

...ad less than adequate support and information
...gement. We've done the best we can, using books and
...uddle through challenges with software, unclear and incon-
...and practically unreadable specifications from the World
...onsortium (W3C), the body responsible for developing and
...many web specifications. As a result, the history of markup for the
...as been quite tumultuous.

...t markup is incredibly important to both designers and developers. The document is the critical piece of the puzzle, best laid in its proper spot between the
visual and the functional. To allow for future innovation and optimal portability,
finding that puzzle piece and snapping it into place is necessary.

Back to the Future

I'm sure many of you are familiar with the basic history of HTML, but for those who are not, I'm going to give a brief overview here. Understanding HTML's history will help you gain perspective as to why working with markup properly is so important.

HTML was developed expressly for the web, which, at the time of its emergence, was a text-based environment. Tim Berners-Lee and his colleagues looked to Standard Generalized Markup Language (SGML)—a meta-language in relatively widespread use for document management applications—for guidance when developing HTML. Because the text-only environment of the web necessitated the most streamlined of markup, HTML was created to be simple and structural.

When the first graphical browser, Mosaic, appeared, the web world was turned on its side, because suddenly information could be presented in a visual context. In ensuing years, browser development began to focus on presentational concerns more than structural ones. This was a heady time in the web's growth, with creative uses of technology appearing practically every day. To accommodate this innovation, much of the structural simplicity of HTML got lost. In fact, HTML was bent and flexed to handle presentation concerns—something it was never intended to do.

The production and proliferation of visual editors added to the loss of structure in HTML, because, by their nature, these editors were concerned with presentation. HTML seemed an afterthought. The goal was to provide the designer with tools to design, and not worry about understanding how HTML works or why it should even work at all. Many designers still take the stance that it shouldn't matter: If the results work as intended, that's the concern—not the structural integrity of the markup.

The complexity of HTML, particularly the use of tables for layout, increased, and until recently, there were no usable alternatives. Interestingly, HTML has shouldered the responsibility of being an integrated technology: HTML has been used for design and for functionality.

For those interested in the advancement of technology, however, looking under the skirts of most web sites is an exercise in frustration. Cascading Style Sheets (CSS), which were introduced relatively early in the web's evolution but still had implementation concerns, emerged to address some of the problems associated with presentational markup. (See Chapter 9: "The Technology of Design: Cascading Style Sheets.") By the time HTML 4.0 was developed, the W3C made a clear cry for the separation of structure from presentation.

Enter XML, which was also fashioned from SGML. XML is very structured, and as a result, the W3C decided to redefine HTML as an XML application rather than that of SGML. This resulted in XHTML, which is used in a variety of ways today. XHTML has opened up many technical opportunities when it comes to document flexibility and interoperability. This is seen quite clearly when we look at the growing interest in wireless access to the web, which, of course, cannot support the complex markup and scripting that we've become accustomed to using.

Because of the lack of support for CSS in older browsers, the problems of presentational HTML (or XHTML) persist. However, because of the vast improvements in recent browsers, there is now a shift in both thinking and action when it comes to dealing with markup. Interestingly, designers and developers alike are beginning to see the rationale of this separation, and designers are especially interested in the greater control that CSS ultimately allows for design.

Structured markup keeps me honest, and actually gives me less to worry about. When I use XHTML-style markup, I don't have to worry about whether I need an ending tag or not. Using both <p> and </p> ensures that the spacing is more consistent. Improper nesting can lead to strange displays as the browser attempts to make the best of a bad situation— proper nesting avoids those problems. After writing a book in DocBook (an SGML and now also XML-based markup), I find it annoying to read and very difficult to write markup that isn't well-formed.

—J. David Eisenberg, author of *SVG Essentials*

The result of this changing history is the same for designers or developers: To manage integration and inspire innovation, web markup needs to be carefully structured and presentation concerns need to be moved to their rightful place—with style sheets.

The Art of Structure

Does this mean, then, that HTML is no longer a concern for designers? In many ways, designers should be much more concerned with and focused on learning and using CSS, because that is an appropriate language for design. Even when used purely for structure, however, HTML and XHTML have an artistic elegance that savvy designers will embrace. After all, having a good foundation is imperative to a design, whether it is a visual anchor point in a painting or the physical foundation of a building. The integrity of that foundation provides the base on which creativity can be built.

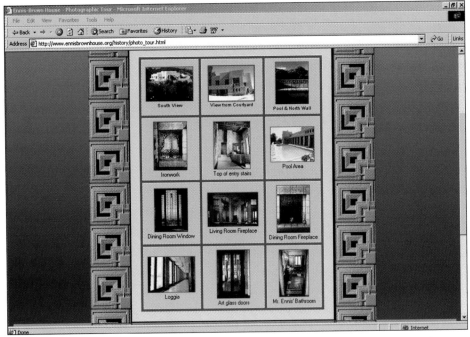

www.ennisbrownhouse.org.

A quick look at the basic structure of an HTML or XHTML document—down to the way elements are named—shows us immediately that there is an artistic, human metaphor. Web documents have a head, and a body. In a sense, markup is the skeleton upon which we will draw the rest of the human figure.

> *The human body is first and foremost a mirror to the soul, and its greatest beauty comes from that.*
>
> —Auguste Rodin

If you think of a document in these more artistic terms, it becomes clear that to forget any aspect of the structure, or to put it in an inappropriate place, renders the figure deformed. To avoid that unhappy problem, the proper structuring of documents is called for.

Museum

I live in a relatively small city, but we have numerous museums and art galleries that I rarely visit. It seems an unfortunate truth that most people don't take advantage of the resources around them. Is there a museum in your town that you haven't yet seen? Or perhaps a gallery? Seek out a museum, and carefully look at the artwork on display. Think about structure—how is the painting or sculpture that you're examining put together? Sometimes the emotional impact of aesthetic expression is found in the elegance of its structuring, and experiencing this can provide you with new inspiration when approaching your web-related work.

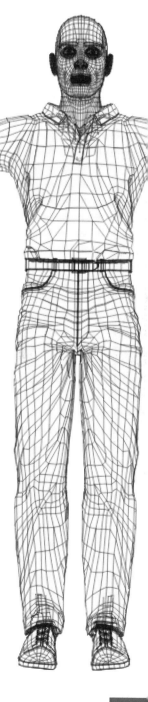

Paintings and monotypes by Joseph Forkan,
www.joeforkan.com.

It's well and good to discuss the theory of structure and how it might relate artistically to human form, but unless you have some practical guidelines, you'll likely be at a loss to know exactly what constitutes a structured document versus one that has been prepared for presentation.

Structured documents do the following:

- Follow W3C recommendations for document requirements

- Contain the proper document structure, including correct DOCTYPE declaration, root element, head and title elements, and body element (or frameset if for a frameset document)

- Validate against the Document Type Definition (DTD) or XML Schema followed in that document

While I won't spend too much time explaining what these individual issues entail, I will step through the creation of a structured HTML 4.01 document with you here. This exercise is important to follow now, because it will provide the basis upon which you'll create a page that is fully integrated with the concepts explored in this book.

To learn more about HTML and XHTML in depth, please see **Special Edition Using HTML and XHTML,** *published by Que.*

Practical Reality: Structuring a Document

Over the years we have seen the technology improve quicker than we can keep track of. In this mad rush, we attempted to adopt the new technologies before really understanding how they were intended to work. Today things have slowed down a bit, and it has allowed us to look at what we have created and see not only the flaws in the technology, but even more so the misuse of the technologies. We are going back to our roots of basic document structure for the sake of portability, interoperability, and even accessibility.

The separation of style from content has been the cornerstone for cost-saving web measures. Those who didn't learn that the content needed to be separated are finding themselves going back and rebuilding a lot of what was already created, in order to develop sites that are, in my words, forward-thinking, meaning that the site isn't just built for what kinds of technologies we have today, it's built for what is to come tomorrow.

—Nick Finck, Editor in Chief, *Digital Web Magazine*
(**www.digital-web.com**)

Jenga

You might have played a game called Jenga (www.hasbro.com). It's popular worldwide. Players begin with a tower made of wood blocks. Each player must remove a block and place it on top of the tower without knocking the tower over. The mental challenge is to follow and understand the changing structure and balance of the tower as its blocks are repositioned. Go play Jenga with some friends, and next time you work with markup, remind yourself of the power structure has over the tower's integrity.

Crowning the Figure: DOCTYPE

Ready to create your structural masterpiece? Great! Begin then with the component that crowns the figure: The DOCTYPE declaration.

The DOCTYPE declaration does the following:

- Denotes which markup language you're using by name and version

- Describes the location of the Document Type Definition (DTD) to which the document will validate

- Allows contemporary browsers to switch to Strict mode, which enables strict rendering of your markup and CSS according to specifications

Depending upon the language you are using, your DOCTYPE declaration is going to be designed somewhat differently. Table 8.1 lists DOCTYPE declarations for use with HTML 4.01, XHTML 1.0, and XHTML 1.1.

At this writing, the W3C web site has several DOCTYPE examples of written with relative URIs, such as simply "strict.dtd" where the absolute URI is needed. These examples are incorrect for usage outside of the W3C site, you need to point to the absolute URI in the DOCTYPE. Those listed here are accurate for general use.

Table 8.1 DOCTYPE declarations for HTML 4.01, XHTML 1.0, and XHTML 1.1

Language Version and DTD	DOCTYPE
HTML 4.01 Strict	`<!DOCTYPE HTML PUBLIC "-//W3C//DTD HTML 4.01//EN" "http://www.w3.org/TR/html4/strict.dtd">`
HTML 4.01 Transitional	`<!DOCTYPE HTML PUBLIC "-//W3C//DTD HTML 4.01 Transitional//EN" "http://www.w3.org/TR/html4/loose.dtd">`
HTML 4.01 Frameset	`<!DOCTYPE HTML PUBLIC "-//W3C//DTD HTML 4.01 Frameset//EN" "http://www.w3.org/TR/html4/frameset.dtd">`
XHTML 1.0 Strict	`<!DOCTYPE html PUBLIC "-//W3C//DTD XHTML 1.0 Strict//EN" "http://www.w3.org/TR/xhtml1/DTD/xhtml1-strict.dtd">`
XHTML 1.0 Transitional	`<!DOCTYPE html PUBLIC "-//W3C//DTD XHTML 1.0 Transitional//EN" "http://www.w3.org/TR/xhtml1/DTD/xhtml1-transitional.dtd">`
XHTML 1.0 Frameset	`<!DOCTYPE html PUBLIC "-//W3C//DTD XHTML 1.0 Frameset//EN" "http://www.w3.org/TR/xhtml1/DTD/xhtml1-frameset.dtd">`
XHTML 1.1	`<!DOCTYPE html PUBLIC "-//W3C//DTD XHTML 1.1//EN" "http://www.w3.org/TR/xhtml11/DTD/xhtml11.dtd">`

To begin your structured document, select the language and language version you are using, and place the DOCTYPE at the very top of your document:

Listing 8.1   Structure Begins with the DOCTYPE

```
<!DOCTYPE HTML PUBLIC "-//W3C//DTD HTML 4.01
➥Transitional//EN"
"http://www.w3.org/TR/html4/loose.dtd">
```

Setting Down Roots: The html Element

Once you've got the DOCTYPE down, it's time to begin the document's structure with the html element.

Listing 8.2 shows an HTML 4.01 document with the root element, and Listing 8.3 shows an XHTML 1.0 document with the root along with the XML namespace attribute for XHTML, which is a required attribute for XHTML documents.

Listing 8.2   HTML 4.01 Document with Root Element

```
<!DOCTYPE HTML PUBLIC "-//W3C//DTD HTML 4.01
➥Transitional//EN"
"http://www.w3.org/TR/html4/loose.dtd">
<html>

</html>
```

Listing 8.3   XHTML 1.0 Document with Root Element and XML Namespace

```
<!DOCTYPE html PUBLIC "-//W3C//DTD XHTML 1.0
➥Transitional//EN"
"http://www.w3.org/TR/xhtml1/DTD/
➥xhtml1-transitional.dtd">
<html xmlns="http://www.w3.org/1999/xhtml">

</html>
```

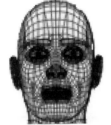

Because XHTML is a reformulation of HTML as an XML application, you can add the XML prolog. The XML prolog allows authors to declare the document as an XML application, as well as specify the XML version, the type of document, and the character encoding. There have been some problems using the XML prolog in older web browsers. Upon seeing it, many browsers will render the contents of the markup as text or not display at all. To avoid this problem, most web designers leave the prolog off at this time.

It's interesting to note that once the DOCTYPE is in place, non-empty elements (those elements containing content) work in a container fashion. In other words, you'll open the html element with the <html> tag and close it with the </html> tag. This container construct has always reminded me of those lacquered, nested boxes where you'd open one box, and another, smaller box was nested in it, and so on. Of course, elements without content, referred to as *non-empty* elements, are single tags without this nesting phenomenon.

Control Center: The Document Head

Just as our brains can be considered our human control center, so the document head can be seen as a means to define meta information about the document at hand.

All structured documents in HTML 4.0 and XHTML must have a head element, and they also must have a title element. The title element allows you to provide a title for the page that will appear within the browser interface, helping users orient themselves to the page and its contents. Other elements, such as meta, script, style, and link can also be used as needed, but the basic structure requires the title element, as shown in Listing 8.4.

Listing 8.4 XHTML 1.0 Document with Head and Title

```
<!DOCTYPE html PUBLIC "-//W3C//DTD XHTML
➥1.0 Transitional//EN"
"http://www.w3.org/TR/xhtml1/DTD/
➥xhtml1-transitional.dtd">
<html
xmlns="http://www.w3.org/1999/xhtml">
<head>

<title>Page Title Goes Here</title>

</head>

</html>
```

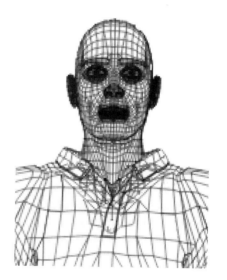

If you truly love Nature, you will find beauty everywhere.

—Vincent Van Gogh

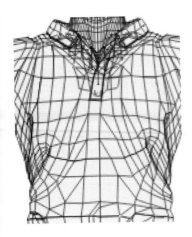

Beauty and Grace: The Document Body

The body element is the portion of the structure responsible for what is displayed in the browser (or other user agent) window. Anything in this section, unless explicitly hidden, will display for your site visitors.

Listing 8.5 adds the body element in container fashion.

Listing 8.5   XHTML 1.0 Document with Body Element Added

```
<!DOCTYPE html PUBLIC "-//W3C//DTD XHTML 1.0
➥Transitional//EN"
"http://www.w3.org/TR/xhtml1/DTD/
➥xhtml1-transitional.dtd">
<html xmlns="http://www.w3.org/1999/xhtml">
<head>

<title>Page Title Goes Here</title>

</head>

<body>

</body>
</html>
```

Listing 8.5 is also a perfect example of a structured document ready to have content added to it.

Structured Content

What you put into your body definitely will appear on your body. The same is true with web documents. To keep the body looking trim, following markup structure conventions is like having a regular workout. You end up with increased strength as well as flexibility.

These conventions also form the basis of how you will address presentation in CSS. Create a well formed HTML or XHTML document, and writing your CSS becomes that much easier.

Headers

If you come from a publishing or design background, you already know the answer to the popular question: Why do headers get physically smaller as their numeric value increases, when font sizes get larger as their numeric value increases?

Headers are a document convention that organizes information in a—you guessed it—structured way. A header level 1 (h1) holds the first position in header hierarchy. Typically level 1 headers are used for the first important headline within the document. Subsequent headers, such as level 2 (h2) and level 3 (h3), are used to denote sub-topics.

Listing 8.6 demonstrates the way headers are properly used. Paragraphs with content would appear between each of these headers; for now, I want you to think in terms of how the headers relate to one another.

Listing 8.6   The Structure of Headings

```
<!DOCTYPE html PUBLIC "-//W3C//DTD XHTML 1.0
➥Transitional//EN"
"http://www.w3.org/TR/xhtml1/DTD/
➥xhtml1-transitional.dtd">
<html xmlns="http://www.w3.org/1999/xhtml">
<head>

<title>Using Headers</title>

</head>

<body>

<h1>Using Headers</h1>

        <h2>Header Hierarchy</h2>

        <h2>Header Syntax</h2>

<h1>Styling Headers</h1>

        <h2>Creating an Element Selector</h2>

                <h3>Choosing the selector</h3>

                <h3>Adding rules</h3>

    </body>

    </html>
```

In publishing, the general convention is that you should have at least two subheads for any top-level header. A single subhead looks awkward.

I've purposely indented each level header in this markup so you can easily see that both level 1 headers are top-level information for the discussion at hand. All level 2 headers detail the top-level information that they are under. Level 3 headers detail the level 2 headers, and so on.

Paragraphs and Breaks

When creating paragraphs, it's good to ensure that the content flows logically, perhaps even rhythmically, for web audiences. Shorter bursts of text are considered the rule of thumb for best readability in a screen environment. Grammatically, a paragraph should contain at least four sentences. The first introduces the thought, any number of sentences within the paragraph should expand on the thought and support it, and the last sentence should sum up your idea. A four sentence paragraph is a nice general measure for web paragraphs, although you can of course use more or less as your needs or design goals dictate.

As you know, paragraphs must be preceded by an opening <p> in HTML and can be closed with a companion closing tag </p>. In XHTML, there are no exceptions: Both the opening and closing tag are used to properly contain the content. Closing any element with content (referred to as a non-empty element) is an intelligent thing to do from a structural standpoint; each paragraph can now stand as a distinct structure within the structure around it.

Line breaks are achieved in HTML with the <br> tag. In XHTML, you use the same tag but terminate the line break according to XML rules: <br />. Line breaks are considered structural, but you should reserve them for those times when you need to break a line to be sure the line is rendered accurately, such as with an address or a poem. Paragraphs are considered block-level elements and, as such, will cause a line break after the element closes. Placing breaks within a block-line element, such as the p element, is a good practice in structure.

> *Closing non-empty elements, such as paragraphs and list items, is a good idea from the point of view of structure, even in HTML, which does not require it.*

Listing 8.7 shows an XHTML 1.0 document with a header, a paragraph, and a break.

Listing 8.7 Proper Use of Headers, Paragraphs, and Breaks

```
<!DOCTYPE html PUBLIC "-//W3C//DTD XHTML 1.0
➥Strict//EN"
"http://www.w3.org/TR/xhtml1/DTD/xhtml1-strict.dtd">

<html xmlns="http://www.w3.org/1999/xhtml">

<head>

<title>Structured Content</title>

</head>

<body>

<h1>Header Level I</h1>

<p>First paragraph of content. This paragraph can
contain as few as one sentence and as many sentences
as you like. However, general guidelines for web
content say keep paragraphs short, like this one.</p>

<p>If you have a difference of opinion, you can phone
your complaint to our complaint department:<br />


500-000-0000</p>

</body>
</html>
```

In the past, many people have used paragraphs and breaks to hack workaround spacing and placement for HTML presentation. This should be avoided.

Lists

Another component used to structure content is a list. You are likely to be familiar with three specific kinds of lists:

- **Ordered lists.** An ordered list is a sequential list.

- **Unordered lists.** A bulleted list, such as this one.

- **Definition lists.** An indented list used for definitions of terms.

Lists also break up content in a structured way, and using lists properly in a document can increase the comprehension and readability of the content. The goal with lists is to use them properly. Ordered lists are best used for any information that is sequential, such as a stepped recipe. A bulleted list is for information that is organized but not necessarily sequential. Definition lists are best used for terms and their definitions.

When it comes right down to it, all web markup should be considered structural.

So What About Emphasis and Strong?

While emphasis and strong do result in changing the appearance of any content contained within its tags, why are they allowed in strict documents?

If these elements are being used properly, simply to mark a word as emphasis, it isn't really considered purely presentational to use them, because emphasis and strong are determined by the browser in terms of the way any content is displayed. As a result, even strict XHTML 1.0 and XHTML 1.1 documents will validate if you use these elements.

Integrated Design

As I mentioned earlier, presentation became a role of HTML, despite the fact that HTML was never intended for the purpose of visual design within a GUI environment. Understanding that there have been difficulties and limitations with browser support for CSS, the W3C offers transitional options in HTML 4.0 and 4.01, as well as XHTML 1.0. These transitional DTDs include elements and attributes used for presentation and, if you are properly declaring the DOCTYPE of your DTD, you can use these presentational elements.

> *Be careful to use only those elements and attributes that are in the DTD, unless you're prepared to write your own that contains them. Proprietary elements and attributes are generally not part of valid markup. An example of a proprietary attribute would be topmargin, which is an IE attribute, not a W3C attribute. Validating your documents with a validator such as is found at http://validator.w3.org/ is an excellent way to ensure that your documents are using only accepted elements and attributes for the language version you're using.*

When you employ presentational markup in HTML or XHTML, you are integrating markup with such design elements as color, space, shape, and type. However, the control you have over these design elements is very limited and typically dependent upon a host of conditions. For example, if you use font size="2" to size a font on your page, that size is different from browser to browser, platform to platform, and resolution to resolution. Although there are still considerations of this nature with CSS, the level of control is much more profound.

In the case of HTML and XHTML, integrating design and technology appears to be ineffective. As a result, the rise of CSS as a critical tool for web professionals is inevitable. To effectively make markup interoperable between platforms and user agents, it ideally remains pure, with other technologies working intimately with it to provide a better basis for integration.

CHAPTER 9

The Technology of Design: Cascading Style Sheets

Web designers must be control freaks: We must control our designs in the best possible way. Web designers must also be Zen Masters. When there is no control, we must go with the flow or suffer the stressed-out consequences.

Cascading Style Sheets (CSS) offer control in ways that HTML or XHTML presentational elements and attributes never could achieve. You are likely to already be working with style, but as with HTML and XHTML, you've also probably learned what you can from web sites, books, and viewing source code.

CSS binds style to structural elements, and *style should follow structure.* This chapter will show you how to create a style sheet from the perspective of the structured concepts learned in Chapter 8. The examples here will help you structure your style sheets more effectively, but even more importantly, provide a new way for you to begin thinking about design.

Structured markup has forced me to design more effectively for online environments than ever before. When designers came online, we put content into HTML tables, images. We used spacer GIFs and sometimes forgot to put in appropriate alt attributes when needed. Now with CSS, we are able to apply style to structured markup without those hazardous HTML workarounds.

We can, have, and should seek out content that is organized and marked up accordingly, while we approach stylizing our pages in a new way with new methods. It is this new way of design, ensuring the content is properly placed before applying a style, that is forcing me to design for the web in new ways and helping me break out of commonplace web page designs.

—Christopher Schmitt, **www.cssbook.com**

CSS: Past and Present

Interestingly, the earliest CSS drafts became available early in the web's innovative life, May 1995. Soon, the CSS1 draft was available, and then on December 17, 1996, the W3C officially recommended CSS1. CSS2, which as of this writing is the current recommended version of CSS, became a W3C recommendation in May 1998.

Designers had the technology they needed to separate presentation from structure, but not the browser support to provide viable alternatives from table based layouts and so on. Over time, designers and developers began to use style sheets for those elements they could more confidently address: fonts and colors.

But, layout remained elusive, and for many people, it still does. Enough browser support exists now, however, that a movement to finally sever the ties with tables as the de facto method for laying out web pages is underway.

How long this will take to proliferate is questionable, because many of the people for whom you design will require consistent presentation with no or only very slight degradation across a range of browsers, including browsers such as Netscape Navigator 4.x, which has only partial implementation of CSS. To address those needs, designers still default to the table-based means of layout.

As more support from Web browsers comes to the fore-front, designers and developers are empowered with two primary levels of control:

- **Site-Wide.** Using linked style sheets, you can control 1 page or 1 billion.

- **Presentation-Specific.** With any variety of CSS, you can control many visual presentation concerns across a single page or many. With CSS, you have a much wider palette when it comes to measurement, color, and positioning methods.

What's more, using a combination of style techniques and multiple pages, you can also target specific browsers and work to ensure that they are able to successfully render your CSS work, make your pages print-friendly, and ensure that your pages gracefully degrade in those browsers that do not support them.

Making the Move to CSS Layouts

I encourage readers to think about using style-based layouts wherever and whenever they can, and learn techniques to gracefully degrade their work for older browsers.

While this seems a difficult thing to do, there are some good books and great web sites that can help you.

Two books from New Riders are well worth a look: Eric Meyer on CSS *(ISBN: 073571245X) and Christopher Schmitt's* Designing CSS Web Pages *(ISBN: 0735712638).*

Cascading Style Sheets: Separating Content from Presentation, *by Eric Costello, Owen Briggs, Matt Patterson, and Steve Champeon is an excellent book for designers to use to gain a better sense of CSS, especially when it comes to layout. (Published by Glasshaus, www.glasshaus.com.)*

As for web sites, I highly recommend a visit to Eric Costello's "CSS Layout Techniques: For Fun and Profit" (www.glish.com/css), Owen Briggs' "Box Lessons" (www.thenoodleincident.com/ tutorials/box_lesson/index.html), and BlueRobot.com's "Layout Reservoir," (www.bluerobot.com/web/layouts).

> *When I say 'structured markup,' it's usually shorthand for 'non-table markup without all those darned font tags.'*
>
> *The biggest improvement structured markup has brought to my workflow has been the incredible ease of editing actual document content. Rather than having to hack my way through a choked jungle of <td> and <font> tags, I can quickly skim through a clean, minimal markup until I find the part I want. I can also alter that structure itself in mere moments, since I don't have to work through a twisted tangle of nested tables. I can just rearrange a few <div> elements, if even that much, and the change has been made.*
>
> *But above all, the switch to cleanly structured markup has freed me from my preconceived notions about what is possible in web design. The combination of simple structure and CSS leads to some surprisingly powerful techniques—the kinds of things that tables could do only with difficulty, or not at all. By leaving the limitations of tables behind, a fascinating new realm of design effects opens up. It's almost like learning to design all over again, but this time with a much more powerful set of tools that are much simpler to use.*
>
> —Eric A. Meyer, **www.meyerweb.com**

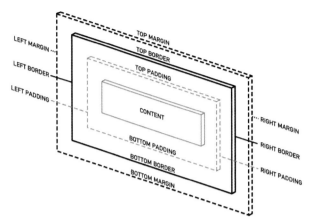

*Figure 9.1   The CSS Box Model. Illustration by Miles Tilman, used
courtesy Christopher Schmitt (**www.cssbook.com**).*

Styling a Structured Document

Many style sheets are written a bit haphazardly, often due
to the lack of structure in the associated web document. To
avoid this pitfall yourself, start with a structured document.
Listing 9.1 provides you with a sample on which to practice
your styling. You'll recognize the structural issues discussed
in Chapter 8. You'll refer back to this listing as we work
through the creation of a complimentary style sheet.

Beware the Box Model

*CSS uses the intelligence within a browser to
control formatting of HTML or XHTML
elements. This is done via the box model.
The Box Model comprises boxes that are
generated by elements within the document's
tree and laid out according to the visual
formatting model. The visual formatting
model allows for the measured display of
information on screen.*

*Figure 9.1 shows the Box Model in its
idea. However, Box Model implementation
has been somewhat different in browsers,
causing page components to appear
differently when using CSS positioning.*

*For more information on dealing with
Box Model concerns, see "Here Be Dragons,"
a problem and workaround set for box
concerns by Owen Briggs (**www.thenoodle
incident.com/tutorials/box_lesson**).*

Listing 9.1 Structured XHTML Template: No Presentation

```
<!DOCTYPE html PUBLIC "-//W3C//DTD XHTML 1.0
➥Strict//EN"
"http://www.w3.org/TR/xhtml1/DTD/xhtml1-strict.dtd">

<html xmlns="http://www.w3.org/1999/xhtml">

<head>
<title>Structured Markup Example</title>
</head>

<body>

<h1>Header Level I</h1>

<p> Lorem ipsum dolor sit amet, consectetuer
adipiscing elit, sed diam nonummy nibh
euismod tincidunt ut laoreet dolore magna aliquam
➥erat volutpat. Ut wisi enim ad
minim veniam, quis nostrud exerci tation <a
➥href="tation.html">ullamcorper</a>
suscipit lobortis nisl ut aliquip ex ea commodo
➥consequat. Duis autem vel eum
iriure dolor in hendrerit in vulputate velit esse
➥molestie consequat, vel illum
dolore eu feugiat nulla facilisis at vero eros et
➥accumsan et iusto odio dignissim
qui blandit praesent luptatum zzril delenit augue
➥duis dolore te feugait nulla
facilisi.</p>

<ol>
<li>Step 1</li>
<li>Step 2</li>
<li>Step 3</li>
</ol>

<h2>Header Level II</h2>

<p>Ut wisi enim ad minim veniam, quis nostrud exerci
➥tation ullamcorper suscipit
lobortis nisl ut aliquip ex ea commodo consequat.
➥Duis autem vel eum iriure dolor
```

```
in hendrerit in vulputate velit esse
➥molestie consequat, vel illum dolore eu
feugiat nulla facilisis at vero eros et
➥accumsan et ➥iusto odio dignissim qui
blandit praesent luptatum zzril delenit
➥augue duis dolore te feugait nulla
facilisi. Lorem ipsum dolor sit amet,
➥consectetuer adipiscing elit, sed diam
nonummy nibh euismod tincidunt ut laoreet
➥dolore magna aliquam erat volutpat.</p>

<ul>
<li>Item 1</li>
<li>Item 2</li>
<li>Item 3</li>
</ul>

<h3>Header Level III</h3>

<p>Duis autem vel eum iriure dolor in
hendrerit in vulputate velit esse molestie
➥consequat, vel illum dolore eu
➥feugiat nulla facilisis at vero eros et
➥accumsan et
iusto odio dignissim qui blandit praesent
➥luptatum zzril delenit augue duis dolore
te feugait nulla facilisi. Lorem ipsum
➥dolor sit amet, consectetuer adipiscing
elit, sed diam nonummy nibh euismod
➥tincidunt ut laoreet dolore magna aliquam
➥erat
volutpat.</p>

<p>Ut wisi enim ad minim veniam, quis
➥nostrud exerci tation ullamcorper
<a href="suscipit.html">suscipit</a>
➥lobortis nisl ut aliquip ex ea commodo
➥consequat.</p>

</body>
</html>
```

As you can see, this document has three heading levels, paragraphs, links, and two types of lists. Figure 9.2 shows the document as it appears in Netscape Navigator 6.2.

Do Everything Backward Day

In order to gain some insight about how structure influences our daily lives, and inspire innovative, creative thoughts of your own, it sometimes helps to do something completely different than you normally would.

So, it's time to take a break and momentarily rebel against logic. What if you were to un-structure a day or structure it differently? Do something out of logical order today: Have dinner for breakfast, or eat dessert before the main course. Enjoy yourself, and don't think too much about it until after, when you can write or draw some of the feelings that came about during the exercise.

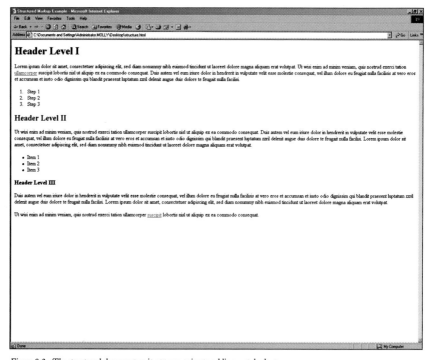

Figure 9.2   The structured document as it appears prior to adding a style sheet.

Styling the Body

Beginning by styling the body element is a good idea, because CSS operates on a concept known as *inheritance*. This means that unless you state otherwise, a parent element will pass on certain features to its child element. So, you'll want to get a lot of your presentational concerns handled in the body element, which is the parent structure to all of the rest of your elements.

To begin your style sheet, open up a text or other editor, and, adding no other elements, type in the element selector body. Then, you'll create some rules for the body, as shown in Listing 9.2.

Listing 9.2 Styling the Body

```
body {
        font: normal 0.9em/1.4em Verdana,
        ➥Arial, Helvetica, sans-serif;
        color: #555555;
        background-color: white;
        margin: 20px 20px 20px 20px;
}
```

The rules I create for these styles are not as important as the point that I am creating a style sheet that is structured using a basic document structure.

Make sure all your element names in CSS, such as body, p, li and so on are lowercase when you are working with XHTML.

Figure 9.3 shows the document with the new styles applied.

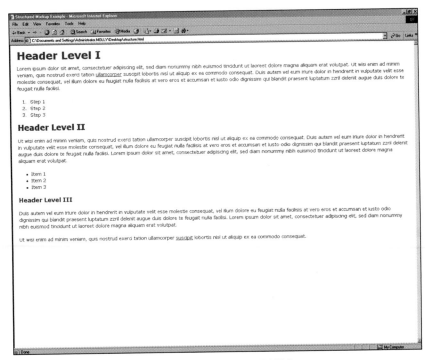

Figure 9.3 Adding style to the body. Note how the style is inherited by all child elements.

Styling the Headers

As mentioned in Chapter 8, headers form a hierarchy of information. Some designers like to call attention to them with a different font face than is being used for body text and to use different colors to discern between the header levels. In this case, I've done both, as you can see in Listing 9.3.

Listing 9.3 **Styling the Headers**

```
h1 {
        font: bold 1.9em Georgia, Times,
        ➥"Times New Roman", serif;
        color: #0000cc;
        background-color: transparent;
        margin-bottom: -10px;
}

h2 {
        font: bold 1.5em Georgia, Times,
        ➥"Times New Roman", serif;
        color: #3399ff;
        background-color: transparent;
        margin-bottom: -10px;
}

h3 {
        font: bold 1.1em Georgia, Times,
        ➥"Times New Roman", serif;
        color: #6699cc;
        background-color: transparent;
        margin-bottom: -10px;
}
```

Figure 9.4 shows the new styles applied to the headers.

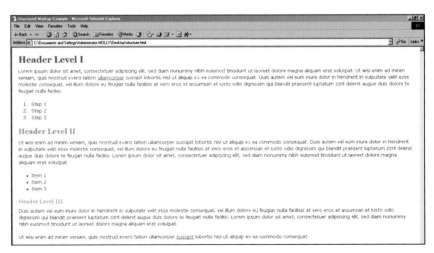

Figure 9.4   Controlling the style of the headers.

Styling Body Text

Body text is the bulk of readable text on your page. Typically, body text should be readable. In simple terms, that means providing some contrast between body text and background, and a reasonable text size.

I tend to choose ems or percentages to size text with CSS. The reason is because you end up with text that is resizable using browser controls. This ensures that people with vision challenges can resize your text and read the content. You can't consistently get that effect using other CSS measurement sizing.

Listing 9.4 shows how I've styled my paragraph, and Figure 9.5 shows the results.

Listing 9.4   Styling the paragraph

```
p {
        font: normal 0.9em/1.4em Verdana, Arial,
        ➡Helvetica, sans-serif;
}
```

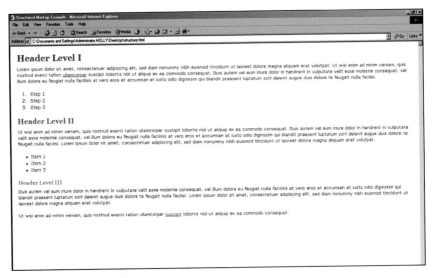

Figure 9.5   Styling the paragraph text.

Styling the Lists

Lists can be styled in a variety of ways. You might wish them to have text of a different color, a special background, or shapes for disks used in bullets. For this example, I changed the color of the font for both the ordered and the bulleted list (see Listing 9.5).

Listing 9.5 Styling the Ordered and Bulleted List

```
ol {
        font: normal 0.9em/1.4em Verdana,
        ➥Arial, Helvetica, sans-serif;
        color: #336633;
        background-color: transparent;
}

ul {
        font: normal 0.9em/1.4em Verdana,
        ➥Arial, Helvetica, sans-serif;
        color: #cc0000;
        background-color: transparent;
}
```

Figure 9.6 shows the markup with the updated style.

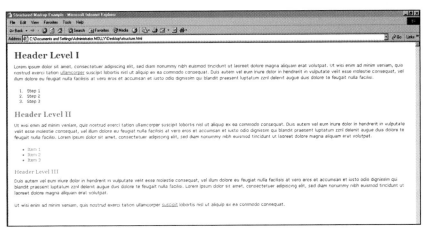

Figure 9.6   List styles.

You may also add styling for the list item (li) element, as shown in Listing 9.7.

Listing 9.7 **Styling the List Item**

```
li {
        font: normal 0.9em/1.4em Verdana, Arial,
        ➥Helvetica, sans-serif;
}
```

Adding styling for both the list type (ordered or unordered) and the list item will ensure that your list styles will be as consistent as possible across browsers. If you leave out one or the other, the style might be missed by a given browser, leaving you with unsuitable results.

Styling the Links

You are undoubtedly aware of the power of CSS and links if you've ever worked with CSS before. Again, the exercise of this chapter isn't to show you the cool things you can do with CSS, but *how* to think about your CSS structure as it relates to your document structure. You'll finalize the exercise by observing how to attach style to the links found within the example (see Listing 9.8).

Listing 9.8 **Styling the Links**

```
a {
        color: #0099CC;
        background-color: transparent;
        text-decoration: underline;
}

a:visited {
        color: #0077AA;
        background-color: transparent;
        text-decoration: none;
}

a:active {
        color: #0099CC;
        background-color: transparent;
        text-decoration: none;
}

a:hover {
        color: #0077CC;
        background-color: #EEEEEE;
        text-decoration: none;
}
```

Figure 9.7 shows the link style.

Link in hover state

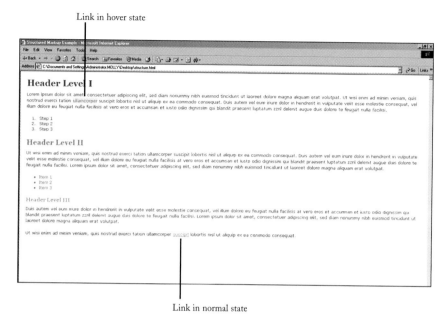

Link in normal state

Figure 9.7 Link styles are added.

Listing 9.9 shows the entire style sheet. Compare the sheet's structure to the structure of the corresponding document, as shown in Listing 9.1. You should easily see how the structure of your style sheet follows the structure of your document. By structuring both this way, you create an incredibly strong foundation upon which you can create designs. You'll also avoid problems generated by haphazard practices, lessening the time you spend with markup and increasing the time you have to actually design!

Listing 9.9 **The Completed Style Sheet**

```
body {
        font: normal 0.9em/1.4em Verdana,
        ➥Arial,Helvetica, sans-serif;
        color: #555555;
        background-color: white;
        margin: 20px 20px 20px 20px;
}
```

continues

continued

```
h1 {
        font: bold 1.9em Georgia, Times, "Times New
        ➤Roman", serif;
        color: #0000cc;
        background-color: transparent;
        margin-bottom: -10px;
}

h2 {
        font: bold 1.5em Georgia, Times, "Times New
        ➤Roman", serif;
        color: #3399ff;
        background-color: transparent;
        margin-bottom: -10px;
}

h3 {
        font: bold 1.1em Georgia, Times, "Times New
        ➤Roman", serif;
        color: #6699cc;
        background-color: transparent;
        margin-bottom: -10px;
}

p {
        font: normal 0.9em/1.4em Verdana, Arial,
        ➤Helvetica, sans-serif;
}

ol {
        font: normal 0.9em/1.4em Verdana, Arial,
        ➤Helvetica, sans-serif;
        color: #336633;
        background-color: transparent;
}

ul {
        font: normal 0.9em/1.4em Verdana,
        ➤Arial, Helvetica, sans-serif;
        color: #cc0000;
        background-color: transparent;
}

li {
        font: normal 0.9em/1.4em Verdana,
        ➤Arial, Helvetica, sans-serif;
}

a {
```

```
    color: #0099CC;
    background-color: transparent;
    text-decoration: underline;
}

a:visited {
    color: #0077AA;
    background-color: transparent;
    text-decoration: none;
}

a:active {
    color: #0099CC;
    background-color: transparent;
    text-decoration: none;
}

a:hover {
    color: #0077CC;
    background-color: #EEEEEE;
    text-decoration: none;
}
```

You may continue adding styles to your sheet as you see fit, and then either link your sheet to the document using the link element or embed the sheet within your document using the style element. If you're using the style sheet to control an entire site, using linked style is most sensible. If you're trying to control a single page within a site, or just a few pages within the site, embedding the sheet is acceptable. Just remember that the primary point here is to keep your CSS in step with your document's structure, which will make both your CSS and your markup a lot easier to manage.

Coloring Outside the Lines

Integration of ideas can best occur not when we focus only on the typical way something is done, but on its opposite. In order to understand how to use dark colors, for example, you need to use light ones as well when you work with design. Innovation often occurs as a side-effect when we're doing something else as opposed to focusing on the details.

You probably colored in a coloring book at some point in your life. Were you the type who was very concerned with staying inside the lines? No matter, it's time to inspire innovation by getting a coloring book and disobeying the rules. Use unusual colors—how about red for the sky, green for stars? Be a rebel: Color outside the lines.

Integrated Design

CSS presents a challenge to web authors. To address the issue of structuring markup, and then refine our practices with CSS, means coming up with a platform upon which new ways of seeing the web can emerge. Because we now have a model where document structure and presentation are completely separate, we can not only integrate the technology of CSS with its design opportunities, but we can integrate our documents with other delivery platforms, including PDAs, pagers, cell phones, WebTV, and so on. When structured properly, our documents also will be more accessible to people with disabilities using such adaptive technology as screen readers and alternative input devices.

CHAPTER 10

Browser-Based Dynamic Technologies

The last two chapters focused on structure and order. It's time to add a little flavor to the soup by looking at what makes up dynamic technology and by learning to think about the functional in aesthetic terms. Although this chapter won't teach you scripting, it will clarify many common scripting terms, and help you gain insight as to the power of scripting from a design perspective.

Perhaps one of the most frustrating problems of our profession is that the terminology we use is confusing and inconsistent. Such words as "dynamic" are tossed around every day, and the expectation is that we truly know what they mean. The word "code" is used to refer to HTML or XHTML, when programmers and document specialists would argue vehemently that markup is not, in fact, code. It is markup, and should be referred to accordingly. Still another problem with terminology is when we refer to W3C specifications as *standards*, when technically speaking they are not. They are *recommendations*.

Confusion has ensued. In this confusion, designers easily might be put off by technical terminology. One such term is *scripting*. What does it really mean?

What Is Scripting?

Scripting is a sequence of code that is executed by an application to process it rather than directly by the computer's processor. In this regard, scripting is decidedly different than a compiled, complex program, which is handled by the computer's processor.

Scripting directly influences ways in which designers can control aspects of their designs via the browser, as well as handling more functional needs, such as managing forms, routing browsers, and so on. When it comes to having control over user input, looking at creative ways to work with navigation, personalization, and animation, scripting takes an important role in the web designer's life.

Because our concern in this book is client-side design rather than back-end technology, the focus here is on client-side scripting. This, in essence, means understanding a bit about JavaScript, one of the many popular scripting languages used for web sites. In the next section you will investigate where JavaScript came from, what it does, where it's going, and how it's used to create dynamic, integrated design.

Dictionary

Becoming more accurate in how we use words can assist us greatly in not only integrating our own skills, but also in more effectively communicating with others in work or social groups. Learning how words connect to ideas is also a good metaphor for the way scripting works with browsers.

If you don't have a paperback dictionary, buy one. Take it with you everywhere you go: the post office, the supermarket, a bar, a party. Any time you hear a word that you are not entirely sure of, look it up—who knows what new words you might (accurately) learn!

Demystifying JavaScript

Many readers of this book, particularly the programmatically inclined, might not need this lesson in clarity and history. But Fear of Programming is a very realistic concern for many designers. Look at JavaScript and how it came to be, however, and you'll find that it's not as mysterious or confusing as you might think.

The JavaScript scripting language evolved from Netscape's LiveScript. Sun Microsystems, developer of the Java language, teamed with Netscape to make some adjustments to LiveScript, and then reintroduced it under the new name JavaScript. JavaScript's arrival was meant to coincide with Sun's release of the programming language Java.

Beyond their names, Java and JavaScript have very little resemblance to each other. Java is a complex, compiled language that can be used to develop entirely standalone applications, as well as applets which work within web browsers. JavaScript is an interpreted language that works primarily with web pages. JavaScript is usually included within the web document or linked to it, and it is processed (interpreted) line-by-line by the browser.

Seven months after the release of JavaScript, Microsoft, having its own interests at heart, released JScript, a version of JavaScript for Internet Explorer. This, of course, contributed to the ongoing browser disparities.

JavaScript is valuable for programmers and designers. The good news for designers is that JavaScript can help you add plenty of cool tools to your pages. JavaScript is great for visual functions, animations, and dynamic page generation, as well as more technical implementations, such as browser detection and forms validation. The designer will especially enjoy JavaScript for such things as

- Creating expanding menus

- Toggling text and images within a page

- Allowing visitors to change the colors on a page

- Offering text-resize options

One of the greatest uses for JavaScript is to work with a browser's intelligence in order to create dynamic pages. But what is dynamic, really? See the section "What is Dynamic" later this chapter to learn more.

> *JavaScript…will be useful to non-programmers, but only for limited, cookbook-style tasks. For better or worse, complete mastery of JavaScript requires sophisticated programming skills.*
>
> —David Flanagan, *JavaScript, The Definitive Guide* (O'Reilly)

What's more, you don't need to out and out learn how to script (although if you're up to the challenge, it certainly can't hurt), because there are plenty of places where you can get scripts to achieve effects from the simple to the complex. Plus, Macromedia Dreamweaver MX, Adobe GoLive, and similar tools offer scripts and script editors that can be very helpful if you're looking to create dynamic designs without scripting.

Of course, if you know nothing whatsoever about JavaScript, look at the following sidebar, "Finding Scripts," to find community support in order to achieve your goals. You'll want to experiment, but you'll also want additional help while getting comfortable with scripting. Until you're comfortable working with scripting, you'll want to avoid using it on commercial sites.

What Is Dynamic?

The first step in gaining a foothold in terms of dynamic technologies is to understand what dynamic means. In simple terms, a dynamic page is one that changes in some way. This change takes place based on user input, some pre-defined scripting, or pre-defined application and database services. Here we will focus on changes that occur based on user input, because that is where designers get to have the most fun.

Think of dynamic design as a highly integrated form of content management and delivery. By combining the strengths of other technologies and managing them with the browser itself, you potentially have a highly efficient means of offering a rich experience to your site visitors. Several technologies contribute to dynamic design:

- **HTML or XHTML.** An HTML or XHTML document and its elements provide the medium.

- **CSS.** Using Cascading Style Sheets, numerous presentational effects can be accomplished.

- **Scripting.** Some form of scripting, such as JavaScript, is used to carry out dynamic events.

- **Document Object Model (DOM).** The interface provided by the DOM is necessary to carry out script-related tasks.

The *DOM* is a means by which browsers (and other software) can give you access to programs and scripts to dynamically modify various aspects of a document, including its structure, presentation, and contents. It's important to realize that markup, CSS, and scripting are combined with the DOM unique to the browser, allowing for the integration of multiple technologies.

The implementation of the DOM in browsers has varied enormously over the past years. This has led to a lot of confusion about how browsers interpret and deal with scripting. (For more details about DOM-related activities and resources, check out **www.w3.org/DOM**.) The DOM is especially important in scripting and the creation of dynamic pages in general, and specifically to what has become known as *Dynamic HTML* (DHTML).

DHTML is somewhat misunderstood. Many professional-level designers think of it as being a language, when in essence, it is a combination of technologies working along with browser intelligence to create dynamic options. The major frustration with DHTML has focused on two main concerns. The first is that the implementation of the DOM from one browser type and version to the next was very different because there was no standardized DOM (and it often remained difficult even after there *was* a standardized DOM), browsers were developed in their own way. The second is that proprietary elements that did not make it into specifications also have caused many authors frustration.

Finding Scripts

Some great script collections are available online. Do note that some of these scripts are for limited use or contain copyright information of which you must be aware. Here are a few sites for your perusing pleasure:

- *Developer.com (www.developer.com). A general resource for software developers and web professionals with good tutorials, articles, and script archives.*

- *Internet Related Technologies (www.irt.org). Another general resource with excellent script archives.*

- *The JavaScript Source (http:// javascript.internet.com). Tons of JavaScript for cross-browser use.*

- *JavaScript.com (www.javascript.com). Cut and paste scripts for just about any use.*

> *Like the web itself, Dynamic HTML is ever evolving. At some point, DHTML may self-actualize and reach its full potential of 'change anything, anywhere, anytime.' It may even change its name—product developers possess a whimsy for this sort of thing—but the concepts defined for modifying elements on a page will necessarily continue to mature.*
>
> —Aaron Weiss, *Introduction to Dynamic HTML*

Combine the changes in scripting languages, browser versions, and different DOM implementations with non-standard authoring practices, and there's a lot of resulting frustration and inconsistency surrounding the creation of dynamic pages.

> *We need not abandon DHTML to build robust, usable, and compelling interfaces.*
>
> —Alex Russell, *DHTML Interfaces: Taking the Next Step*

Despite these problems, however, dynamic design remains a major interest for many, and it can be tapped into by designers who seek to create more interactive designs. As you can see, it's not an easily tackled subject, and will require more research and practice than provided in the context of this book. But, with an understanding of what these technologies are, why they are, and some of the challenges that might exist with them, you're armed and ready to dig deeper. See the following sidebar, "Finding DHTML Sources," to help you explore.

Dynamic Gallery

From hierarchical menu systems to games to advanced animations, scripting can help you be extremely innovative with your visual work. A great way to spark your own creativity is to check out how other designers are implementing scripting and dynamic design. The sections that follow contain inspiration for menu systems, games, and animations.

> *Not all the dynamic designs here are cross-browser compatible.*

Menu Systems

Scripting is especially good for creating menu systems that break from the ordinary.

As you can see in Figures 10.1 through 10.4, **www.milonic.com** uses DHTML to create a simple but effective menu system.

Finding DHTML Sources

As for JavaScript, many online DHTML archives exist. Just be sure to read the terms of use for the sites and their scripts. Here are a few samples for your enjoyment:

- *WebReference DHTML Lab (www.webreference.com/dhtml). Tutorials and scripts.*

- *DynamicDrive (www.dynamicdrive.com). Tutorials and scripts with recommendations and FAQs.*

- *DevX DHTML Zone (www.devx.com/dhtml). Articles, tutorials, help, and tons of DHTML scripts.*

- *DHTML Central (www.dhtmlcentral.com). Dynamically driven DHTML developer's site.*

- *BrainJar (www.brainjar.com). Very progressive DHTML with plenty of options and guidance for designers.*

- *Scottandrew.com (www.scottandrew.com). A full library and script repository for the contemporary dynamic designer.*

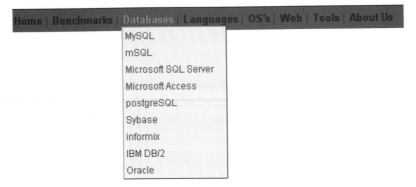

Figure 10.1 *The menu at rest.*

Figure 10.2 *The menu with a CSS link hover.*

Figure 10.3 *A submenu expanded.*

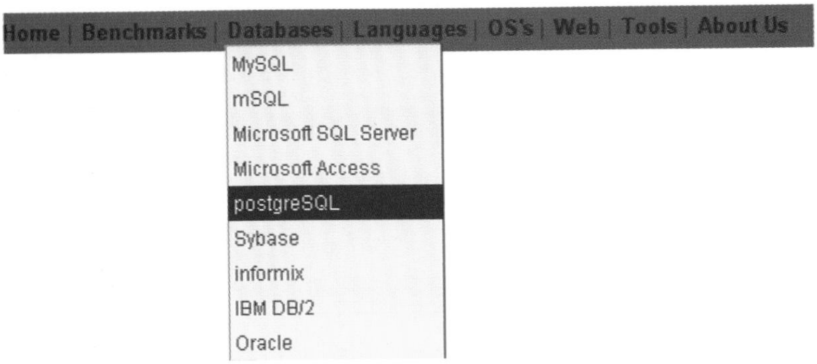

Figure 10.4 *A submenu choice highlighted upon mouseover.*

The menu on **www.brainjar.com** uses DHTML to mimic familiar soft-ware menus (see Figures 10.5–10.7). Note that the site author uses these demos along with valid XHTML.

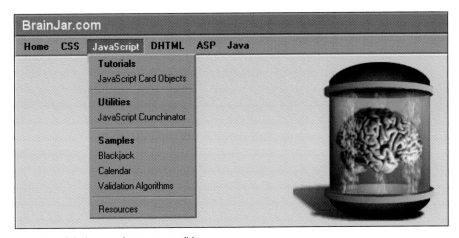

Figure 10.5 *The menu at rest.*

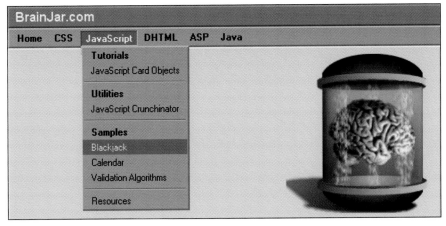

Figure 10.6 *Bringing up a submenu on mouse click.*

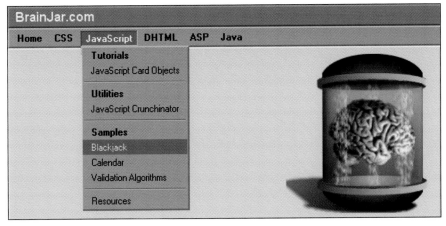

Figure 10.7 *Submenu choices highlight on mouse over.*

The visually elegant DHTML menu of Project Seven
(**www.projectseven.com**) was created with extensions for
Macromedia Dreamweaver (see Figures 10.8–10.10).

Figure 10.8   The menu at rest.

Figure 10.9   Bringing up a submenu on mouse over.

Figure 10.10   Submenu choices highlight on mouse over.

Games

While not specifically an aid to visual design, games can add entertaining options to your site. Using scripting you can create some great games, such as the checkers game shown in Figures 10.11 through 10.14. You can try it out at **www.lostjungle.com/games/dhtml/checkers/**.

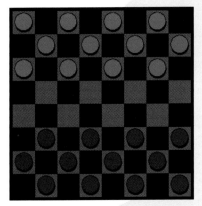

Figure 10.11 The checkerboard.

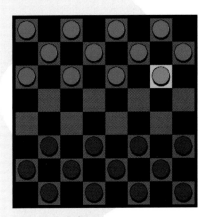

Figure 10.12 I select a piece.

Figure 10.13 Moving the piece.

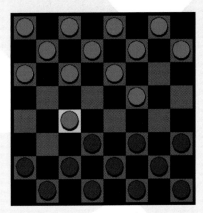

Figure 10.14 The computer responds with its own play.

I liked the hangman game at **www.manythings.org/hmjs/ animals.html** for its practicality. (See Figures 10.15 and 10.16.) The game teaches English as a Second Language students how to improve their spelling.

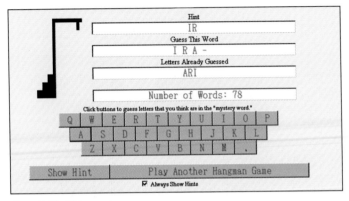

Figure 10.15   Adding a guess.

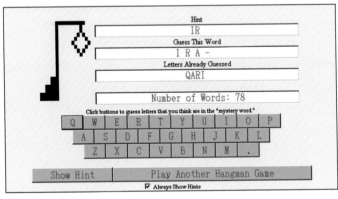

Figure 10.16   The game responds.

Animations

Scripted animations are often complicated but quite beautiful.

For example, I just get a kick out of the BlobbyCopter animation at **www.p-richards.demon.co.uk/ blobbycopter/blobbycopter.htm**. It is scripted in DHTML. (See Figures 10.17 and 10.18.)

Figure 10.17 BlobbyCopter begins flight.

Figure 10.18 BlobbyCopter on the move.

The extremely sophisticated look to the Titanic animation at **www.p-richards.demon.co.uk/titanic/titanic.htm** might make you think it was created with Flash. No, it was done with scripting. (See Figures 10.19 and 10.20.)

Figure 10.19 The image at rest.

Figure 10.20 The story begins to be told, with various elements on screen changing color and position. Audio has also been added to the design.

Stereo

Music is by its very nature an integrated expression. It is mathematical, it is artistic. The authoring of music is much like scripting—fitting components together in a way that creates a dynamic end result is the composer's goal.

Try listening to at least three musical compositions from vastly different genres. You might try a good tenor aria, a country song, and a hard rock tune. Listen carefully to the structure and artistry within the song itself, as well as between songs. How are they alike? Different? What does listening to these songs and words make you think and feel?

Integrated Design

As you can see from the last two examples, dynamic delivery of content is completely within reach within certain contexts and certain browsers. This disparity has hurt scripting (and DHTML specifically) in a lot of ways, especially as newer media technologies are developed.

Still, when you examine how DHTML itself is a technology that relies on the integration of markup, CSS, scripting, *and* the DOM interface within browsers, it isn't difficult to conclude that mastering any combination of these skills can bring you closer to having many exciting options to achieve innovative, interactive results.

CHAPTER 11

Emerging Integration Media:
Flash, SVG, SMIL

As we forge ahead with structured markup, CSS, and the creation of a standardized DOM, we'll find that we are indeed empowered to work with and use web technologies in innovative ways. In fact, several technologies are coming to the forefront that are inherently integrated in that they combine scripting, markup, and multiple forms of media, such as text, video, animation, and audio.

The three integrated technologies of greatest interest at this time are:

- **Flash.** Really, I mean the SWF file format and not the program from Macromedia, although certainly Macromedia Flash is the most sophisticated SWF generator on the market.

  Flash is not an emerging media, you say? True, Flash has a strong foothold on the web due to its longevity. A recent deepening of the scripting features in Flash tools and outcries from critics who are upset with the lack of accessibility in Flash are bringing about changes that in some ways do place Flash into an emerging technology category.

- **SVG.** Scalable Vector Graphics expresses the intelligence of scalable graphics using XML. Markup generates images and animations instead of more traditional binary files.

- **SMIL.** The Synchronized Multimedia Integration Language synchronizes and integrates multiple forms of media.

All of these technologies rely on plug-ins to work. Flash has gained significant distribution over the years, and since major companies have an interest in SVG and SMIL (Adobe and Real, respectively), their potential for future implementation and wider-spread use is great.

Play Cranium

Multimedia may be the most integrated of all areas in web design because it brings together a variety of skills. If you're looking for a break and want to try a game that taps into your use of multiple skills, try a game called "Cranium." Cranium makes players do all kinds of integrated activities to win. For more information, see www.playcranium.com.

Flash in the Can

The only successful web technology that has been developed with designers truly in mind is Flash. To understand what I mean, look at the way contemporary designers have been trained. If you came to the web from a visual design background within the last ten years or so, you're probably used to working with visual tools.

The argument is really as simple as that. Flash is a visual tool. Markup, scripting, and other language-based technologies have few viable options when it comes to entirely visual editors.

What Designers Want

I've already discussed the concern most trained designers have with control. When it comes to visual design, designers—especially those from a print background—do not think of the web right away. Instead, they open Adobe Illustrator, Quark, and Adobe Photoshop, or a similar grouping of vector, layout, and graphic editing tools. They use scanned objects, photographs, color, typography, and filter effects, combining them in some elegant and still appropriate way to bend for the web when the time comes.

This is the way it generally breaks down:

- Illustrator lets you work with complex shapes and integrate type into a design.

- Photoshop is the consummate tool for working with graphic elements and tapping into the power of history and layers to give your work flexibility.

- Quark lets you refine layout and work with margins, text placement, text flow, and white space.

Most designers will be very familiar with this trio of tools, or a similar grouping including FreeHand, PageMaker or InDesign, and Corel.

Whatever the tools, designers use them to create unusual and interesting layouts *without* thinking of the constraints that markup imposes. The act of designing with such tools is at first a visual process—a process that is, as you are by now well aware, unstructured and, therefore, very different from writing markup.

Designers, especially those who come from a print background and who are accustomed to pixel-by-pixel design, want that elusive control, whether it's over font size, margin measurements, specific positioning, or real color. You undoubtedly already know that achieving these things with web markup and related technologies can be very challenging, particularly if you're designing for a wide audience using a variety of browsers.

> *About 99% of the time, the presence of Flash on a website constitutes a usability disease.*
>
> —Jakob Nielsen, Alertbox

The question then, is how to balance this ongoing need for the control found in contemporary design tools with effective markup.

Flash and Markup

I'm a web standards evangelist. Flash is fraught with problems, especially in terms of accessibility and integration with standards. But Flash has also been a huge part of the visual beauty of the web. As such, I'm going to play devil's advocate a bit and show *why* Flash is such a good fit for designers. But my ultimate argument is to get readers to become *integrated*. This means loving Flash for what it can do, but also relying on markup, CSS, and scripting as well.

The lines are being drawn in the sand. For many designers working on the web, Flash is the be-all and end-all of design options because it provides the interface, and the tools environment as described earlier, that a designer is sincerely interested in and comfortable with. However, today's contemporary web is filled with progressive markup and transitional technologies that have those individuals more comfortable with code, concerned about standards, and concerned about accessibility very excited. There are advantages to each, really, and in order to best integrate as a designer *and* developer, it helps to walk over those lines in the sand and gain an understanding of both.

Because visual designers tend to work in the visual world, many have eschewed hand-authoring HTML or XHTML and are relying instead on popular visual editors, such as Dreamweaver or GoLive. This isn't necessarily a bad thing—particularly as certain programs are becoming more sophisticated and inclusive of W3C ideologies. But for the time being, using visual editors successfully requires you to have both an understanding of markup *and* the design tool in question.

Even the most sophisticated visual editors demand that users have a pretty hefty knowledge base. If you use the grid or visual layout editors in GoLive or Dreamweaver, for example, your markup will be much heavier than if you understand something about working with tables and use a combination of your knowledge and the visual editor's interface to achieve your results. What's more, without a deep understanding of contemporary markup goals—accessibility, separation of presentation and document structure, and globalization—you'll have more trouble producing documents that look good, function fabulously, and adhere to W3C recommendations.

So What About CSS?

Part of the problem (say it with me) is that HTML was never meant to be a language of design. Even with CSS, I dare you to get successful margin control, consistent fonts, positioning of visual elements, and application of color or background graphics in a strict environment. Right now, you can't do it and be fully interoperable across browsers, browser versions, and platforms. You can come close. You just can't have ultimate control. And, you're not supposed to. In fact, true innovation often comes about when you have the opportunity to see limitations as advantages, and find new ways of doing things. For this reason, I encourage all readers who have stuck to Flash as opposed to digging deeper into what can be done with markup and CSS to look more deeply into CSS. This will help you gain a better perspective of how, and why, Flash is so ultimately appealing to large groups of web designers.

When the entire world has browsers that can successfully support every feature of CSS, we'll be happy campers. Well, mostly. Learning to write sound CSS is a serious commitment. And as this entire book points out, what works for many visual designers isn't necessarily what works for the more programmatically inclined, and vice-versa.

Until someone develops a fully visual interface that writes proper and efficient CSS, it's hard to wedge CSS into a visual designer's workflow. That means CSS, while built for designers, isn't yet the effective design tool designers would ideally like it to be. Fortunately, such tools are becoming available, leveling the playing field a bit. Style Master, from Westciv.com (**www.westciv.com**) is the first visual interface for style sheets. It's a great start, but it's a long way from where we need it to be. Another tool, TopStyle, from the developer of the original HomeSite tool, is working hard to expand the TopStyle program to provide visual interfaces for CSS.

Scripting

DOM-related scripting definitely offers an array (if you'll pardon the pun) of options for designers. This is especially true when we want to create interactive events from simple mouseover graphics to sophisticated games.

Though scripting can truly empower a designer, it suffers from the same interface problems as CSS and markup. Sure, you can grab free scripts all over the place, but that's a haphazard way to build a professional application, especially if you don't understand enough about a given script language to troubleshoot problems. And, the same interoperability issues exist, especially with DHTML, as you examined in Chapter 10. Remember, too, that some site visitors turn off JavaScript, and it's not hard to understand why most scripts aren't built for those individuals who are uncomfortable with programming.

Flash, of course, gives visual designers who don't want to program a lot of ammunition with which to create dynamic sites. But things get even more complex when we throw ActionScript into the stew. Suddenly, Flash designers find themselves encouraged to understand something about scripting, because they can do so much more with Flash as a result. So, by nature, Flash is becoming an integrated technology. Still, if you want to use it well, you'll obviously need to beef up your knowledge of programming and become more integrated in your skills.

Flash and Emerging Design Techologies

But what of such technologies as Scalable Vector Graphics (SVG) and Synchronized Multimedia Integration Language (SMIL), and how they relate to Flash? Aren't these technologies geared in many ways toward visual people? Yes, they are, and they're both growing in terms of support and tools, as you'll read later in this chapter.

SVG is particularly interesting because of its scalability, its language-based structure, and—most especially in the context of this discussion—the fact that visual tools are being built for it as the technology is designed. Several major applications, including CorelDraw, have or are adding SVG export filters. Batik, an open-source toolkit for SVG developers, is also a promising solution. Designers can work in a visual editing environment, and the applications generate impressively sophisticated markup.

There are a few problems with SVG, however, the foremost being that it requires a specialized plug-in of which most site visitors are unaware or are not interested in installing. This differs dramatically from the Flash Player, which comes installed with the browsers used by most site visitors. And, although animations are on the horizon for SVG, the technology still needs time to grow.

SMIL's current state of affairs is similar. The technology as a whole is exciting for designers, because the focus is not only on design elements, but also a rich selection of interactive multimedia: text, images, sound, and motion. All of this is in a development environment that's somewhat accessible, yet demands a fairly high learning curve and balance of skills. In order to use SMIL, you have to use a combination of design and programming skills. You have to be integrated. Flash can demand this, too, but doesn't *necessarily* demand it.

So where does this leave us? From a visual design perspective, the Flash format and its related tools are the only tools currently capable of providing a *completely* visual development environment and a wide choice of how to employ the technology. I could leave the argument there, but of course that doesn't address the very serious limitations that Flash has in terms of accessibility and cross-platform compatibility.

As you probably know, Flash produces and controls color, text, layout, shape, and motion. What did I say designers want? Control! Well, Flash gives it to them, and then delivers the product to the web.

Reading through that virtual ton of letters received while writing an article on this subject for *Web Techniques Magazine*, I naturally came across quite a few from readers who were extremely opposed to Flash. Some argued that Flash was inaccessible, inappropriate for the web, and that the plug-in issue remains a concern. And they're right, all of these things are true. While Flash has come a long way from its early days by adding ActionScript, and now, with Flash MX, is beginning to address concerns with accessibility and usability, it still has a long way to go.

> *There's one more thing about Flash that can't be denied: Flash content is inaccessible to blind and otherwise disabled users. Back when Flash was all about animation and motion graphics, Flash accessibility wasn't all that important. But Flash has evolved into an environment for building complete web applications. Indeed, a growing number of sites are being built entirely in Flash.*
>
> *To disabled users, these sites are saying, 'We don't want your kind here. We don't need your business. Go away.' That bothers me. If Barneys department store was to remove its handicapped ramps and bathroom grab handles, it would be sued. But its inaccessible web site wins awards.*

—Jim Heid, Heidsite, **www.heidsite.com**

On the other side of the fence are the enthusiastic designers who love the visual interface and the control Flash affords, even over motion design. This is great, and I advocate it where more conservative standards proponents will not. However, I do so with a major caveat: Use the appropriate application where it's appropriate. You're not going to use Flash on a site designed for blind people. Similarly, you will likely use Flash when you want to create very sophisticated interfaces and motion design for a piece of progressive art.

> *Were Saul Bass alive today, I feel sure he would be using Flash as his creative medium. You only have to look at his stunning titles for movies like Psycho (lines slashing across the screen) and Vertigo (hypnotic spirals) to recognize his work as the forerunner of many of today's Flash web site sequences.*

—Brendan Dawes, *New Masters of Flash*

Now, am I advocating the complete abandonment of markup and putting a copy of Macromedia Flash in everyone's hands despite its accessibility concerns?

Of course I'm not.

Despite my strident opinions on web markup, adherence to recommendations, support for accessibility, and the separation of document formatting from presentation, I still maintain that there's a place for the Flash approach. This is especially true now that Macromedia is adding accessibility features into Flash's development tools.

Really, the most empowered designer will be the designer who can choose between any of these technologies for the right circumstances. That's not an easy decision if you don't know the strengths and weaknesses of both, or if you're not fluid enough in programming and markup to venture into other technologies. So while I believe that Flash is currently the ultimate comfort tool for the visual designer, and I use a devil's advocate approach by supporting it here as equal to or even better than markup technologies for most designers who prefer to work in visual interfaces, I must maintain that in order to be most effective, you'll need to work to integrate all of these skills.

Furthermore, web professionals must clearly understand their audiences and a site's intent, and they must follow that up with the proper blend of integrated approaches to a given design and development challenge. Ultimately, the appropriate form of communication must drive the site. These simple issues—not the preference of one technology over another—are where the trouble lies.

Those who are so convinced that Flash is evil and unusable are wrong. Flash fanatics who are unwilling to look at other means of achieving an end are also wrong.

As with all sensible solutions, the answer lies not in the technology, but in its appropriate use. This means that as a designer or developer you *must learn to integrate* the benefits of Flash with the benefits of markup and emerging accessibility techniques to make your sites as integrated as possible and as sophisticated as is ideal.

For more information about accessibility initiatives at Macromedia, see www.macromedia.com/ macromedia/accessibility.

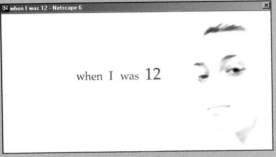

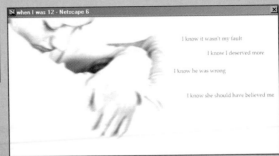

"When I was Twelve":
http://homepage.mac.com/dafitza/flash.html.

It's been called the Flash Killer.

Any time a technology comes out with "killer" attached to it, one must kick back for a moment and question which portion of that perspective grew from an understanding of the technology, and which part was simply the faulty imagination of a marketing department somewhere. Many times, as with SVG (and even more so with SMIL), the technology has all the potential, but is not yet ready for prime time because of the additional technologies, such as plug-ins, that are required to make it work.

But overall, with SVG, I'm willing to be happily surprised. After all, XML was first lauded as being the HTML killer. And, it has succeeded. There will be no future versions of HTML. Instead, XML and its applications have come to the forefront.

What's interesting and important to note is that SVG is an application of XML. Via markup, graphic images, animations, and interactive graphics, designs can be created and implemented for web viewing. Of course, browsers must support the technology, which is one reason that many developers haven't looked into it too seriously— or perhaps haven't heard of it at all.

But think about this carefully. If this whole book is about helping designers and developers think about an integrated approach to the difficult job of professional web site creation, any time we encounter a technology that is *in and of itself* integrated, we need to sit up and pay attention. Even if the technology fails, there are some inherent issues that need to be examined.

SVG is being developed under the auspices of the W3C. As a result, much work is being done to make it compatible with such standards as XML, XSLT, CSS2, DOM, SMIL, HTML, and XHTML, as well as give it sufficient accessibility options via the Web Accessibility Initiative (WAI). In this sense, SVG is a living example of integration.

SVG

To check on current status and ongoing events regarding SVG, please see the SVG news page at the W3C (www.w3.org/ Graphics/SVG).

SVG Concepts

Perhaps the most important concept to grab when studying SVG is that it is *scalable*. This means that graphics are not limited by the fixed nature of a pixel.

Like vector graphics, a scalable graphic can be made larger or smaller, without destruction of the graphic. This is especially important for designing across resolutions. Scalable graphics adjust to the available screen resolution. This alone makes SVG very attractive to designers, as it solves one of our most frustrating issues: Creating designs that are as interoperable, yet visually rich, as possible.

> *Whereas Flash was ostensibly an authoring tool in search of a format, SVG is exactly the opposite. It's a format in search of authoring tools.*
>
> —David J. Emberton, "The SVG Beast in Builder's Flash Point,"
> **http://builder.cnet.com/webbuilding/pages/**
> **Graphics/FlashPoint/082800/index.html**

SVG elements are based on standard graphic design elements. They are

- **Geometric shapes.** A line, a combination of lines, a curve, a combination of curves, or a combination of curves and lines.

- **Text.** Characters and combinations of characters.

- **Raster.** Also referred to as *bitmapped* images. Raster graphics are those that are mapped to bits. This means that they do not contain scalable methods. Raster graphics are typically used in combination with scalable graphics and are composed of photographs and specialty filters.

SVG follows other techniques familiar to graphic designers. The rendering of SVG is based on a paint model. Color, gradients, and patterns are painted onto the screen to gain the end results. Shapes and text can be filled or stroked. Other graphic techniques, such as masking and opacity, can all be applied.

SVG allows access to scripting and to the DOM, which is how SVG supports animations and interactive graphics. This is particularly interesting to me because again, herein lies an example of a task that requires deep integration: combining visual skill with scripting skill.

The interesting aspect to SVG is that the scalable methodology is rendered via an interpreted ASCII language (see Listing 11.1). The exception to this is whenever a bitmapped graphic is used within an SVG environment, the image is included using the SVG image element.

Listing 11.1   The XML Template Structure Used for SVG Documents

```
<?xml version="1.0" standalone="no"?>

<!DOCTYPE svg PUBLIC "-//W3C//DTD SVG
➥20000802//EN"
  http://www.w3.org/TR/2000/
  ➥CR-SVG-20000802/DTD/svg-20000802.dtd>

<svg width="100%" height="100%">


</svg>
```

Browser support is currently sketchy in terms of inline support without a plug-in. Table 11.1 lists support information for SVG.

Table 11.1   General Browser Support for SVG

Browser	SVG Support
Microsoft Internet Explorer	With a plug-in only
Netscape Navigator	Plug-in only
Mozilla	Some support in certain Mozilla builds
Opera	With a plug-in

The browser limitations are certainly an issue with SVG. As time goes on there will be more support for SVG, both from browser manufacturers and from makers of popular software.

To learn the detailed syntax of SVG, please see the specification, available at **www.w3.org/TR/SVG.**

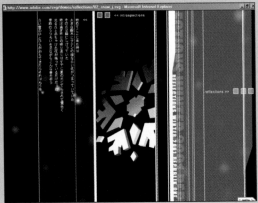

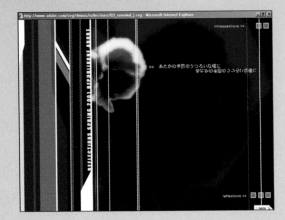

www.adobe.com/svg/demos/reflections/.

Smile, You're Integrated *and* Synchronized

SMIL, the Synchronized Multimedia Integration Language, integrates media using XML.

With SMIL, you can

- Position multimedia elements

- Synchronize the media elements so that audio, video, and text will play at the point you determine

- Customize media so that it plays back to site visitors according to their preferences profile

As with SVG, a big hurdle to overcome with SMIL is that a player currently is required, so the technology, while ready for *you* to investigate, is unlikely to solve any needs you have for your existing commercial projects. Still, integrating multimedia with XML in such a sophisticated way is pretty exciting to those of us seeking strength in visual and technical web skills.

> *As Flash becomes de rigueur, multi-media site builders will need to find a new way to separate themselves from the pack. Enter SMIL.*
>
> —Steve McCannell,
> "SMIL: Multimedia for the Masses,"
> **http://hotwired.lycos.com/webmonkey/
> 00/41/index4a.html**

The largest supporter of the SMIL initiative appears to be RealNetworks, as they are using SMIL to synchronize a variety of their streaming media formats. This support can ultimately be very influential. Apple is also integrating SMIL into its tools, such as QuickTime.

Because SMIL is an application of XML—just like XHTML—you'll notice a lot of syntactical rules that are familiar. Some SMIL rules are

- Elements and attribute names are written in lowercase.

- All empty and non-empty elements must terminate properly.

- SMIL files smust have the SMIL extension at the end: .smi or .smil.

Listing 11.2 shows a bit of SMIL.

Listing 11.2 SMIL Sample

```
<smil>
    <head>
<layout>
<root-layout width="320" height="240"
    background-color="white" />
<region id="ed_button" left="0" top="20"
    width="125" height="22" />
</layout>
        </head>
        <body>
<img src="ed_button.gif" alt="button"
    region="ed_button" dur="2s" begin="2s" />
        </body>
</smil>
```

Times Square or Bust

If you've never been to Times Square in New York City, find some fairly recent pictures of it at night and look at how the multiple forms of media are integrated right into the structures surrounding it. Actual buildings are the projection medium upon which the media is expressed. Times Square is a perfect, larger-than-life example of structure, sound, color, type, space, shape, and motion all integrated to result in a very innovative, very powerful experience.

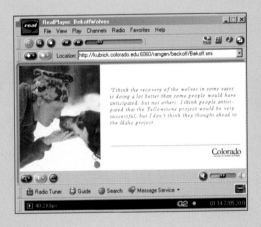

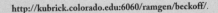

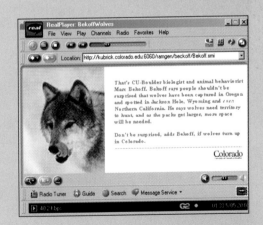

http://kubrick.colorado.edu:6060/ramgen/beckoff/.

Integrated Design

Flash, then, can be seen as a designer's tool that also can demand clever scripting skills. As such, it leans toward being a primarily aesthetic environment. To create innovative sites with it, however, you'll need a technical touch.

SVG and SMIL are particularly intriguing to those individuals seeking to integrate skills and approach more thoroughly. Both technologies are based in language, XML. If SVG and SMIL reach their ideal success potential, we will have some excellent alternatives when it comes to integrated, web-based options.

Index

online script resources, 163
as turned off by some site visitors, 180
use of, to resolve fixed-width design
  problems, 74
uses of, in web design, 161

The JavaScript Source (web site), 163

JavaScript.com, 163

Jiong.com, as example of integrated design, 119

JScript (Microsoft version of JavaScript), 161

Juxtinteractive.com, typographic interest of, 114

K-L

layout
  Cascading Style Sheets (CSS), as alternative to
    tables, 143
  fixed-width designs, pros and cons of, 73-75
    WebTechniques.com, as case study, 77-78
  placement of objects, critical concepts for, 71
  tables, 74, 124
  of web pages, as comparable to that of
    stores, 71

Layout Reservoir (web site), 143

light
  absorption of, as generating color, 52, 57, 60
  diffraction of, 57
  as electromagnetic radiation, 52-53
  energy, characteristics of, 52
  as generated by heat, 53-55
  luminosity, as emission of, 52-53
  refraction of, 57
  sensitivity to, by human eye, 52
  spectrum of, 53-55, 59-61

LiveScript, 161

luminosity (emission of light), 52-53

M-N

Macintosh, Internet Explorer 5.0 for, 42

Macromedia
  Dreamweaver, 123, 162, 168, 178
  Flash, 175, 181-183

markup, structured. *See* HTML

McFadden, Jody (online community management
  specialist), 38-39

memory, nonlinear nature of, as metaphor for web,
  26-29

menu systems, created using DHTML, 165-168

Meyer, Eric A. (Netscape Communications), 40-41
  on advantages of Cascading Style Sheets
    (CSS), 144
  approach to web design, 41
  Eric Meyer on CSS (book), 143

Microsoft
  Internet Explorer
    *proprietary attributes, use of, as
      problematic, 140*
    support for SVG, 187
    version 5.0 for Macintosh, 42
  JScript (Microsoft version of JavaScript), 161
  Macintosh Internet Products Unit, 42

Milonic Solutions web site (dynamic menu systems),
  165-166

monochromatic (one-color) palette, 56

Morton, Jill, 59-60

Mosaic (browser), 4, 124

Mozilla (browser), support for SVG, 187

MSN, 38-39

negative space (whitespace), 79

Netscape Communications, 40, 161

Netscape Navigator
  support for Cascading Style Sheets (CSS), 143
  support for SVG, 187

O-P

online communities, 39

Opera (browser), support for SVG, 187

PDAs (personal digital assistants), designing for, 71

Photoshop, Adobe, 45, 176-177

plug-ins, 176
  for Macromedia Flash, as accessible to most
    web users, 181
  as required for Flash, opposition to, 181

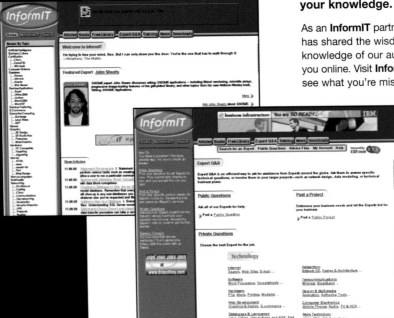

OUR AUTHORS

PRESS ROOM

| web development | design | photoshop | new media | 3-D | server technologies |

EDUCATORS

ABOUT US

CONTACT US

You already know that New Riders brings you the **Voices that Matter**.

But what does that mean? It means that New Riders brings you the

Voices that challenge your assumptions, take your talents to the next

level, or simply help you better understand the complex technical world

we're all navigating.

Visit **www.newriders.com** to find:

► 10% discount and free shipping on all purchases

► Never before published chapters

► Sample chapters and excerpts

► Author bios and interviews

► Contests and enter-to-wins

► Up-to-date industry event information

► Book reviews

► Special offers from our friends and partners

► Info on how to join our User Group program

► Ways to have your Voice heard

New Riders

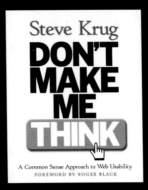

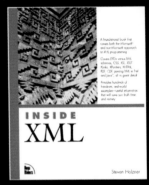

VISIT OUR WEB SITE

WWW.NEWRIDERS.COM

On our Web site you'll find information about our other books, authors, tables of contents, indexes, and book errata. You will also find information about book registration and how to purchase our books.

EMAIL US

Contact us at this address: **nrfeedback@newriders.com**

- If you have comments or questions about this book
- To report errors that you have found in this book
- If you have a book proposal to submit or are interested in writing for New Riders
- If you would like to have an author kit sent to you
- If you are an expert in a computer topic or technology and are interested in being a technical editor who reviews manuscripts for technical accuracy
- To find a distributor in your area, please contact our international department at this address. **nrmedia@newriders.com**

- For instructors from educational institutions who want to preview New Riders books for classroom use. Email should include your name, title, school, department, address, phone number, office days/hours, text in use, and enrollment, along with your request for desk/examination copies and/or additional information.
- For members of the media who are interested in reviewing copies of New Riders books. Send your name, mailing address, and email address, along with the name of the publication or Web site you work for.

BULK PURCHASES/CORPORATE SALES

The publisher offers discounts on this book when ordered in quantity for bulk purchases and special sales. For sales within the U.S., please contact: Corporate and Government Sales (800) 382-3419 or **corpsales@pearsontechgroup.com**. Outside of the U.S., please contact: International Sales (317) 581-3793 or **international@pearsontechgroup.com**.

WRITE TO US

New Riders Publishing
201 W. 103rd St.
Indianapolis, IN 46290-1097

CALL US

Toll-free (800) 571-5840 + 9 + 7477
If outside U.S. (317) 581-3500. Ask for New Riders.

FAX US

(317) 581-4663

Colophon

Integrated Web Design was laid out and produced with the help of Adobe Acrobat, Adobe Photoshop, Adobe Illustrator, Quark XPress, and Microsoft Word on a variety of systems. With the exception of pages that were printed out for proofreading, all files—text, images, and project files—were transferred via email or FTP and edited onscreen.

All body text was set in the Futura family; all headings and figure captions were set in the ACaslon family. Code and markup were set in the Letter Gothic family. Symbol and Sean's Symbol were used throughout for special symbols and bullets.

Integrated Web Design was printed on 60# Influence paper at C.J. Krehbiel Company in Cincinnati, Ohio. Prepress consisted of a PostScript computer-to-place technology (filmless process). The cover was printed on 12pt paper, coated on one side, at Moore Langen Printing in Terre Haute, Indiana.